Tending to the Sacred

Tending to the Sacred

Rituals to Connect with Earth, Spirit, and Self

By Ashley River Brant

sounds true
BOULDER, COLORADO

Sounds True
Boulder, CO 80306

Published 2021

Cover design by Tara DeAngelis
Book design by Linsey Dodaro

Printed in the South Korea

Library of Congress Cataloging-in-Publication Data

Names: Brant, Ashley River, author.
Title: Tending to the sacred : rituals to connect with earth, spirit, and
    self / by Ashley River Brant.
Description: Boulder, CO : Sounds True, [2021]
Identifiers: LCCN 2020041496 (print) | LCCN 2020041497 (ebook) | ISBN
    9781683646785 (hardback) | ISBN 9781683646815 (ebook)
Subjects: LCSH: Self-actualization (Psychology) | Mindfulness (Psychology)
    | Nature--Psychological aspects. | Spiritual life.
Classification: LCC BF637.S4 B685 2021 (print) | LCC BF637.S4 (ebook) |
    DDC 204/.46--dc23
LC record available at https://lccn.loc.gov/2020041496
LC ebook record available at https://lccn.loc.gov/2020041497

10 9 8 7 6 5 4 3 2 1

Contents

Preface

Upon waking I gaze at the sun slowly peeking up from behind the redwoods. I am reminded of the power, light, and pure energy it provides, awakening my being to honor the day. My only intention for this day is to love. I write down my dreams and decode the messages of Spirit and my subconscious needs and desires. I make a cup of tea with the energy of my love, adding a dash of rosewater and a few drops of rose flower essence to uplift my heart, and mindfully step to the west of my home to listen to the flowers. I whisper good morning to the rock roses and sweet peas who dance so playfully in the light wind coming off the coast. I ask that their medicine support me in my day as I become— closer to my truth, closer to my love.

Some of my oldest childhood memories are of speaking with the flowers. This was my first intentional ritual. The soft, sweet-smelling roses, the bougainvillea and orchids that hung above my head, and of course, the intoxicating gardenias that always brought the biggest smile to my face and warmth to my heart. They reminded me that I was safe, that I was home, and that I was sacred, just like them. They reminded me to stay open when things were scary and I had no control in the flow of my life as a child.

I grew up in eleven states, a new school each year, and tossed around among various caretakers. Home was placed behind walls that housed physical and verbal violence and abuse with freshly punched holes that echoed in my heart. The element of the river also seemed to follow me along my winding path wherever I ended up. She taught me the most. I saw myself in her waters—sometimes calm, sometimes thrashing, but always flowing forward and carrying a current of knowing. My connection to the Earth kept me grounded during what was otherwise a tumultuous childhood that lacked all the presence and peace I prioritize today. It was my connection to that which is sacred, to the Earth and Spirit's ethereal guidance, that taught me to survive.

My ears have always been attuned to Spirit for as long as I can remember. Some may call me a medium, but I call my abilities *sacred listening*. It was this connection to the Sacred that led me away from the limitations of my trauma and toward the love and purpose I so desperately was seeking—the dreams burning within. And it did. It also led me to love, to this book, and to you.

I grew up off and on with a grandmother who taught me much about intentionality and how that matters with the energy of our spaces, what we wear, who we spend time with, how we treat each other, and how it all ripples out into the energy field around us. She taught me about divination, the language of the stars, and beauty. We were powerfully close in my youth—a soul bond I don't think I could ever replicate in this life—so when she was no longer around in my later teen years, I felt a gaping hole inside me. It felt like all the light in life was gone and the Sacred along with it. It was her unconditional love—the brightest light I had ever felt in my life at that point—that was blocking out the pain of my childhood traumas, and the absence of her love allowed the overwhelming darkness to wash over me (and my healing to begin). Her passing left me grief-stricken, detached, and searching.

I left art school and moved from the American South to the Californian coast. The land out west was, beyond all logic, calling me to heal and connect to my gifts, and that's when I slowly began my path of ritualistic healing work. It's no coincidence that I would return to these lands ten years later to birth this very book. I believe that ritual finds us in times of profound seeking, even if we don't know what we're looking for. We just know it's out there. We find ritual to connect closer to our truth: what is real within, and without. From the indigenous peoples who danced for the rain, baptisms meant to purify and bring one closer to God consciousness, and all the altars of offerings to the divine beings of all cultures and religions in this world to bring forth healing to their people. We can't help but seek what we feel is missing, and sacred ritual can help us find exactly what that is and guide it home to our hearts.

Before I began my path of ritual healing, I was a fast-food loving, festival-going, binge-drinking, drug-taking American teenager who went barefoot to parties, smoked American Spirit cigarettes like a chimney, and forgot all about intentionality or the Sacred. This was because I completely shut off from it. My spiritual gifts and energetic sensitivities were overwhelming and I was in pain that I wasn't ready to face. An open heart meant my already heightened sensitivities were amplified, and I was afraid of what was on the other side of my openness. I saw and heard spirits, ghosts, and voices on the regular. I could feel the pain of others without even trying. I could feel the suffering of the Earth. It was all too much. So I shut off from feeling everything—my body, my heart, my sensitivities, my connection to others, the language of Earth and Spirit. I didn't yet have the tools, awareness, or guidance to support me on a path of healing and becoming fully embodied in my gifts.

Then, right before my twentieth birthday, I dove in. Whatever I came across on my path, I tried it—EFT tapping, breath work, yoga, vegetarianism, tarot and astrology (with books inherited from my grandmother), manifestation, herbal remedies, crystal healing, plant medicine, energy healing, even praying to goddesses. For years I tried everything and anything to bring me closer to the Sacred and whatever it was I was seeking. Even dropping out of college for the second time to follow the "White Witch of Rock and Roll" (Stevie Nicks) around the country, spending all my student loan money on platform boots and concert tickets, because dancing and singing to her music brought me just a little closer to what I was really seeking: love, courage, passion, freedom, and boundless self-expression.

Little by little, I did move closer to my truth, my desires, and my purpose, but I was also getting closer to my darkness. My pain, wounding, trauma, shadow, fears, and false beliefs were no longer hidden inside of me—everything was sitting at surface level, right in my face for me to witness. I eventually developed food allergies, was sick constantly, found myself enduring one hard lesson after the other, and began to mirror my childhood traumas with the relationships I was attracting. I disconnected from ritual work altogether for a little over a year. I was lost in it all—overcome with decades of unprocessed fears and emotions and unable to find my footing.

I hit complete rock bottom and found myself in a dark night of the soul at twenty-five, following a traumatic car accident overseas where I realized I had lost everything I valued: myself, my boundaries, my love, my passions, my home, my connection to my path, my purpose, and Spirit. Until one day a couple of weeks after my accident, I carried my wounded body out into nature and decided to connect to the Sacred with a simple ritual. I was sitting on a rock at Castle Hill, New Zealand (a place the Dalai Lama has reportedly called the "spiritual center of the world"), and I felt the pull. I took a few deep breaths, set my intention from the truth of my heart, called upon Spirit's guidance, and completely surrendered to my sacred listening. A wind came up suddenly and carried the biggest bee I had ever seen to my hand.

In my youth, my grandmother and I would sit on our balcony in New Orleans watching bees drink from our blooming azaleas and discuss their beauty, symbolism, and magic. In that moment at Castle Hill, I felt my grandmother with me—her love, her wisdom, and her guidance streaming through me. One of the things I've always loved about bees is that they aren't exactly built to fly, with their tiny, delicate wings and round, denser bodies. Not only do they fly, but they hold our world together—servicing a greater mission for all species, guiding us to increased connection, and providing all life on Earth with so much healing medicine.

Like bees, most of us aren't built for success, either. We don't always start off with the resources, knowledge, understanding, and physical support we need to pursue a path of purpose. But when we look within our hearts, we know our truth, brightly burning within, and awaiting our recognition. When we can anchor into that truth, we can fly despite what we were given. Bees remind us that we are all here to serve from the heart, to see our role in this great collective becoming, and fulfill our purposes by working hard against our self-perceived limitations.

I held that sweet Spirit message of love in my heart and I remembered. Like lightning, I suddenly knew the pathway forward. I remembered the knowing within my own Spirit. I remembered my interconnectedness to all that is. The bee in all her graceful strength reminded me of all that is Sacred. I remembered that I am the creator of my life. I remembered that I, too, can fly, despite my trauma, my conditioning, and my fears. I remembered that all I need is already within me, and that I am fully supported on my path.

Right then, I decided to dedicate myself to listening to Spirit, to tending to all that is Sacred, and to showing up for the truth in my heart every single day, with ritual as my bridge. I committed myself to caring for the Earth, my purpose, myself, and my connection to Spirit, and my life was forever changed. Ritual awakened the sensitivities I had hidden away in fear and I found myself suddenly aware of all that was not in alignment with my truth and my soul's purpose for being here. I began purging everything from my life that didn't foster my core desires and truth—relationships, jobs, fears, false beliefs and stories, people-pleasing behaviors, pretending to be someone I was not, and so on. I used ritual to create the clearings, set my intentions, and call on the Sacred for support. Six months later, I decided to no longer hide my gifts and birthed my Soul Tattoo® practice of ritualistic intuitive tattooing, connected with soul family, met the love of my life (my now husband), and the rest is history. Ritual was the bridge that guided me home.

Ritual helps us connect to the otherworlds, to the infinite potentials that exist in the unseen that require the power of the heart to open to. Ritual helps us access all that is within our inner world—made up of shadow and light—and carries us into progressive levels of consciousness to uncover what we are seeking above all: love. Ritual reminds us that love is within us and that all we have to do is honor it. It wasn't exactly my conscious understanding when I began this work as a teenager, but ritual taught me how to heal myself, see myself, empower myself, express myself, and most of all, love myself. The more you see yourself, the more you see the world from a lens of truth, recognizing the interconnectedness of all and the ways we are all here to tend to that which is Sacred.

We are all here to root down into ourselves and awaken to our truth, to our divine power. Tending to the Sacred requires surrender and allowance, allowance for roots to grow, minds to rest, and energy to take on different shapes as we become closer to truth and all the love that is already within us. No matter where we come from—no matter what our conditions, histories, programming, and wounds are—the path for us all is in our sacred tending. It is how we collectively change the world.

These seeds in my spiritual evolution were planted with those roses, gardenias, orchids, bougainvilleas, and bees from my youth, and the river always carried them back to me. Today, with my tea with a hint of rose magic and love in my heart, I dance to remind my body it is a vessel for my Spirit to flow. I place my hands upon the Earth to remind the Earth I am here tending to her needs too, grounded and focused, surrendered to the flow. I leave offerings to my ancestors and spirit guides to feed their energy, which feeds my heart. I remember to breathe to listen to my inner spirit as it guides me. I remember that life responds to how I greet it in each moment. Today, choosing passion over rationality, love over fear, freedom over restriction, spiritual truth over identity, oneness over judgment. Today, leading through love, healing through joy, honoring every challenge, every opportunity that is leading me right where I need to be. I will honor this moment. Because it is sacred. Because I am sacred.

Like my realization following my experience with the bee at Castle Hill, this book came through me like lightning. I wrote it nonstop over the course of a week, staying up most nights writing until my eyes burned and awakening early the next morning to dive back in. Most nights I even wrote while dreaming. Spirit spoke to me clearly and quickly, my ears ringing with insight and encouragement from the spirit beings I walk with—my guides and allies along my path. I tended to the Sacred with my ritual practices along the way to clear away fears around my expression, fears of being seen, fears of being heard and respected, especially because the feminine voice has been silenced and suppressed for thousands and thousands of years. I used ritual to remember who I am when fear crept in, and I used ritual to ground in my heart, anchoring into the love, intention, and purpose of writing this book. I also used ritual to draw in the otherworlds closer to me, to support me in this endeavor.

This book contains rituals and teachings that awakened in me through my connection to Spirit over the last ten years as it grew with my commitment to my ritualistic sacred tending. Many of the rituals were shared with me by the Earth herself, as well as the spirits of the elemental world, with whom I am closely connected and serve as a channel for with my work. I have shared these practices with thousands of people over the years, and they are all practices I weave into my daily life. They have changed my life in more ways than I could express, and they've done the same for countless people I've worked with, bringing them closer and closer to the Sacred.

Most of my clients find a radical awakening through our work together, recognizing their healing power, creative potential, and intuitive awareness, as if veils have been lifted from their eyes and they can now see clearly through the heart of love. Many have gone on to start their own healing arts practices, calling their dreams into the palms of their hands, cultivating spiritual community, and making life shifts that have transformed their realities, relationships, and careers. They enjoy closer relationships with Spirit, feel more guided and supported on their paths, and are not afraid to claim the connection.

This work is done with the unseen. It requires trust in yourself, trust in Spirit, and trust in the potential of what is possible. You'll find evidence of the work in your heart, in the essence of your Spirit. At its root, this work is simply claiming spiritual sovereignty, remembering the wisdom and power already within you, and stepping fully into your power. Not power in the way we see it modeled for us in the modern world, but true spiritual power. The power of love. This work is encoded within you. This book is just a pathway to remember.

You can read the book straight though, or flip to a chapter you connect with at this time on your path. I personally love to work with books as a divination tool by closing my eyes and opening to a random page, and then using the ritual or information on the page as medicine for my healing on that day or week. Take what resonates with you, leave the rest. I hope as you make your journey throughout this book and deeper into yourself you discover all the love and blessings that are within you and this beautiful and wild life. Because you too are sacred.

Introduction

Ritual (noun):

a ceremony or action performed in a customary way

R itual is in our bones. It is encoded in our DNA as an integral way of being. Our ancestors all over the world understood the importance of rituals in daily life, and they practiced them for initiation, atonement, purification, connecting to the elements, to each other, to Spirit, oath, dedications, and honoring of life.

Rituals are not dependent on religion or any set belief system, although we have seen them show up in this way throughout history as rites of passage and blessings, to mark an event in time or bring a community together. Through religion we have also seen stigma and limitations attached to ritual work, which has created strife and division. All rituals, no matter their origin, tend to the Sacred in their own way—the same truth and intention with compassion at its core. This common thread unites us all on our spiritual paths. Ritual predates any religious structure. Ritual at its core is about connection to our own version of God: the higher power of what we feel inside. We discover faith and place the anchor of our hearts into it, without needing to label it in any way. This higher power is not outside ourselves.

All life and its people and experiences are spiritual by nature in all their mystery and connection to the universal. Ritual brings us purpose and connection to the Sacred—the holy essence present in all living things: love. Ritual at the root is a ceremony of the heart, a conversation between the Earth, Spirit, and you. Ritual guides us to create a ceremony of each moment in life. Ritual gives us a sense of belonging to something greater, acting as the bridge that guides us home to the Sacred, merging our inner and outer worlds, bringing magic into the ordinary, and awakening the eternal. Ritual offers us an oasis in time. A space to connect, restore, remember, and reaffirm.

As human beings we are naturally designed with the drive to create stability. This is part of our design to value safety and our basic needs. But as a collective we have let our fear of instability—scarcity thinking—programmed by the world in which we grow up in, have control of this divine power. We have forgotten the essence of this gift and instead have created structures that bind us instead of setting us free to flow safely along our life paths. We form unhealthy habits and routines as a way to have control in our lives and feel safe, failing to see that we are leading ourselves further away from the Sacred.

And our culture thrives off this fear, this alienation—from our spirits, from our hearts, from nature, and from each other. Out of this fear, we listen with desperate ears to dogma that promises to make us "better," more in control, more acceptable, worthy, and successful, but it only ends up separating us further with judgment and shame, silencing our aches for connection and purpose, creating holes of emptiness within. We lose our connection to all that is sacred. Control and its need for power are afraid of stillness and connection to the unknown that ritualistic tending offers, but in stillness we find more power than we could ever imagine. The fog between our hands reaching out for one another, the broken bridges collapsed under pressures to conform to what society says is worthy, puts a focus on all that is missing, when we all just want to belong—to another, to the Earth, to community, and most of all, to ourselves. This connection can only be formed from connection to the Sacred: the love within us and the love that exists all around, in all beings, in ether, and within the Earth.

Ritual work is the bridge that guides us home to the Sacred. Our love is the most sacred, precious thing on this Earth. We find this love by diving down into our own holes and aches, deep in the seeking and wandering that led you to pick up this book. We find home by going against all we were taught that makes us feel *less than*, letting go of all that we believe to be true that blocks us from living a life of bliss and total self-acceptance, falsities fed to us by the capitalistic, patriarchal world we live under. We find home by reaching within and honoring our core desires for pure, loving truth.

We practice rituals in our everyday life without even knowing that we're doing so. Shaking a hand or hugging in greeting, sitting down for dinner with loved ones, washing our hands, taking our dogs for walks, making coffee in the morning, and even saying good night to a family member each night. But the loss of the Sacred and disconnect from our hearts has turned ritual into a mindless routine. Making our coffee in the morning turns into a moment to worry about all our daily *to dos*. Weddings—a sacred rite and celebration of loving union between two beings—become stressful events. Meals become grab-and-gos from one place to the next, or are eaten while multitasking or on our phones. In contrast, mindful ritual offers the structure we crave in a sacred and healing way that allows inner security, stability, and peace to flow effortlessly in grace as the world turns and life changes before our eyes with each passing season.

It's important to remember that our bodies are not machines designed to move throughout our lives in a linear way. We are multidimensional, organic energy here to empower ourselves to co-create with the Universe and embody the love that we all are. With noisy and often chaotic modern lives filled with stressors that take us away from this essence of truth, rituals can remind us of the trust and sacred agreement between ourselves, the Earth, and Spirit. You can think of ritual as spiritual nourishment for the soul. Ritual helps us find inner harmony and perspective, it connects us back to what is true, and it brings us to a sacred space of peace within, beyond the stresses and worries of everyday reality. It enriches our lives, fosters our own inner healer and authority, and ignites an ancient fire within: a spiritual fire that has always been there, carried forward generation after generation and lifetime after lifetime as a desire to connect to something greater—something sacred.

Before we go any further, here are some notes on ritual work to remember:

◇ Ritual can be simple—as simple as mindfully putting on your favorite cozy sweater because it reminds you of warmth and love, lighting a candle, placing your hands upon the Earth or your heart, taking an intentional breath, or expressing your gratitude to another. Cooking can be a ritual, as can singing, writing, listening to music, and even cleaning the house. Ritual can be done anytime of the day anywhere you are. It can be loud or silent, still or with movement. It can be done alone or in groups, day or night, once or thirty times a day.

◇ Ritual is of the heart, not of the mind, so don't overthink it. Perfection is a myth. Ritual means anchoring in the heart and freeing ourselves from the control of the mind.

◇ Ritual is healing. It is a form of self-healing and self-transformation. It's also important to know that healing work is subtle and that our journeys of spiritual evolution are ever unfolding. We don't connect to ritual to reach a certain destination, manifest our dreams overnight, or become automatically enlightened. Despite what you may have heard in new age spiritual rhetoric, the end goal for everyone is not a specific Buddha-esque enlightenment and you don't get there in just one way. Healing rituals are not merely crystals and flowers; healing can be a messy, unpredictable journey. We practice ritual to discover, remember, re-center, and return to love along our winding paths. Ritual is a continuous practice, not a quick fix or one-time thing. It is a way of life. Patience with our healing journey and ritual practice is essential. Healing work takes courage and dedication. It requires devotion to loving yourself and the desire to grow. Start off by being proud of yourself for prioritizing your healing and growth by picking up this book.

◇ Ritual is slow. Slowing down is the only way we can return home to ourselves. Taking breaks and being still are not celebrated in our society (in fact, they can often trigger shame, low worth, or the feeling of being lazy), but we are celebrating them throughout this entire book. Rest and sacred pauses are a huge part of this work.

◇ There is no right or wrong way to conduct a ritual and your rituals can vary from day to day. Ritual above all is a personal practice. It is a sweet tending to your individual needs. At the core of your ritual practice is your heart, and you are here in service to its love, offering it whatever feels good to you. Ritual gives you the tools and freedom to take responsibility for your life. Never act from a "should" place or force yourself to follow any rules that don't feel right for your unique spirit's needs. All the rituals in this book can be modified to meet your needs. What matters most is that the four pillars of ritual work are there, which we will get into in chapter one. Listen to what is calling to you, which rituals feel expansive and nourishing, and notice which rituals you feel resistance to as well (and why). All these feelings will guide you toward a practice that is uniquely fulfilling for your unique wild heart. Trust your process, trust the Universe. Everything that happens as you dive deeper into yourself is for your spiritual evolution, guiding you home to your love.

◇ Ritual works best with commitment and consistency. We cannot expect radical change to occur without consistent effort and dedication from our hearts. Most of the rituals in the book work best when connecting to them again and again, learning and growing as we go, and becoming stronger and more powerful with each sit.

◇ Allow yourself to change. We are creative beings designed for endless change. Know that your practice will evolve as you evolve. What works for you one month may not work the following. This is a sign of growth. If one ritual you connected to strongly at one point isn't supporting you at a later time, that is okay. You will know if it is time to move on to something else. You will have enough ritual tools throughout this book to always connect to something that clicks for you. It's important to have daily, weekly, monthly, or seasonal check-ins with our inner needs and desires to see if they are being met. If something isn't working, we always have the power to change it. Experimentation will be your ally in this journey, especially in the beginning.

◇ When we create change in our daily life, we create a shift in our whole reality. Sometimes change can stir up a lot within our nervous systems—old emotions, fears, stuck energy, or patterns that no longer serve us. Letting go of control and creating space for sacred pauses and tending within allows new energies to emerge. That can feel frightening, but the reward, I promise, is so worth it.

GROUNDWORK

Chapter One

The Four Pillars

R itual work is our groundwork. It offers us a way to bring the spiritual into the physical and ground our souls into our bodies on this Earth. The four pillars that are the foundation of ritual work are intention, space, love, and belief. These pillars are essential ingredients in creating your ritual practice. Without intention, your energy and ritual would lack focus. Without space, they would have no room to move. Without love, your energy and ritual would remain lifeless and easily dissolve. Without belief, you would have trouble connecting to what you are creating. When we gather these pillars together, magic happens— our rituals come to life, energy transforms, healing takes place, and the Sacred responds.

Intention

Routine instantly turns into ritual with a single intention. Intentions set the tone of our ritual practices. They guide the energy of the moment and the type of energy we create. Intention fosters intimacy with Spirit and enhanced awareness and meaning in our lives. Without intention, our rituals may feel lifeless, mindless, ineffective, or disconnected. But it is through our dialog (with ourselves, with the Earth, and with Spirit) that intention is formed and energy is directed toward our ritual. Where we place our intention and attention is always where we place our energy.

It's important to know that every word that falls from your mouth is a spell unfolding. Words are powerful, and language is a universal gift that assists us in creating. The magic incantation *abracadabra* is from the Hebrew phrase *avra kehdabra* which translates as "I will create as I speak." However, intention doesn't always have to be spoken out loud to be powerful. Your intention can be said in your mind, written down, or simply visualized or felt. If your intention is to embody love, you can say so, or you can simply visualize or feel into the energy of love. That could look like picturing someone you love most in this life, visualizing a pink glowing heart floating around you or from within, or bringing your attention to your body and feeling the energy of love in your heart space. When practicing ritual, always take time to find clarity on your intention and feel into what arises. Your intention can be anything you wish to attract, feel, release, create, or embody within. When creating your intention, simply ask yourself the following questions:

How do I want to feel? What do I want to create in this moment? Why am I connecting to this ritual?

You can bring intentionality into everything you do in order to create more ritual, magic, and purpose into your day-to-day life. The purpose of intention is to cultivate meaning in the mundane. This creates a relationship between action, feeling, purpose, and presence. From this relationship, our life grows in meaning. Practice reflecting on how you can create more intention throughout all of life's little moments to bring meaning to the forefront of your life. Here are some examples of simple daily practice rituals:

- ◇ When making coffee or tea in the morning, simply place your hands around your mug and whisper to yourself, "May this bring me vital energy and clarity to navigate my day."

- ◇ When washing the dishes, set the intention to clear the energy of the day from your hands (which are an extension of your heart), thus having the ability to clear any emotional tension you are carrying.

- ◇ Set intentions of vitality and nourishment as you make your meals. Try thinking about how you want to feel when you add each ingredient and what medicine it will bring to you. All food is medicine.

- ◇ Speak to others with the intention to share and connect, and listen with the intention to learn and receive from a nonjudgmental state.

Space

A big part of coming home to ourselves is creating space for our healing. We must honor the sacred space and time we create for our ritual practices. What you create space for in your life takes up space in your life. Tending to the Sacred not only requires space, it deserves space. You deserve space. Space empowers presence. If you have a full day in front of you, begin this work by scheduling just five to ten minutes of ritual time in a way that creates the most ease. Maybe that means waking up five minutes earlier or cutting down on your phone and computer time for the day. If you have time for media, you have time for ritual. Do what works for you and your life, but prioritize your connection and re-centering—not as a daily chore, but as an essential for your balance and well-being.

What takes up space around you in your life also takes up internal space, so this is something to consider when beginning a ritual practice. Everything in your life—friends, the color of your bedroom walls, the food you eat, and your environment—has the ability to change your energy and affect your internal energetic space (emotions, mental energy, health/vitality) and auric field (your spirit body—the subtle energy extending within and around your physical body). As you connect more to your ritual practice, you will slowly begin to notice how everything affects your energy and become aware of what takes up space in your life (in both positive and negative ways). This is important to take note of along your journey, for if something takes up a lot of space in your life and doesn't feel aligned or make you feel happy, it will block new energies connected to your intentions from entering your life.

You may want to carry a journal around with you and just begin to notice what happens when you hang out with a certain person, when you complete a particular task, when you spend an extra twenty minutes in ritual, do something you love, do something different, or let go of control for the day and wander around just following your intuition. Notice what things cause anxiety, fatigue, and fear, and what things light you up, inspire you, make you feel centered, and fill you with joy. All of these energies take up valuable space. The former are contractive energies and the latter are expansive. When we can be more conscious of the energy we invite into our sacred energetic spaces, we can move toward greater alignment on our paths.

We clear and create more space by letting go of the things that take up too much space. This can be an internal energy (such as an old emotion that we are holding onto or a past wounding), a physical energy (a person, object, job, or place that is weighing us down), an unseen energy (such as a belief), or an energy you may have absorbed from a person, place, or event.

Ritual is a powerful tool for clearing space. Clearing space can assist in attracting what we are seeking to connect with in our ritual. Wafting the smoke of a dried plant ally, putting on soothing sounds, and connecting with your breath are all powerful rituals in themselves you can connect to in just a few minutes to create more space in your day.

Here are some tools to help you clear space:

◇   **Plants.** Plants have been used to create space for millennia upon millennia. One of my favorite rituals is to sit with my beloved rosemary bush

at the entry to my house and ask for her
energy to clear my own. I like to clip off a
few sprigs and brush my entire body with
the plant, starting from the soles of my feet
up to my head, as I breathe deeply with the
intention to clear out any energies I
am holding that need to be released.
Another way I like to create space
is to burn a tiny bit of bark from
my favorite trees—cedar or cypress—
and intentionally waft the smoke around my
aura, home, and sacred spaces with my hand or a
found feather. All plants have medicine and powerful energy to offer us. We see the use of herbs such
as white sage and palo santo trending in modern times
and even sold in corporate stores, and both are said to
clear out negative energy. While yes, these are beautiful
energy clearers to create space, this type of usage is the
opposite of sacred Earth tending (more on this in the
next chapter) and these beautiful allies are now on the
bridge to extinction. These plants have been used with
sacred purpose by their indigenous land tenders for centuries. It is of utmost importance to obtain our herbal
allies in sustainable and conscious ways, and work with
herbal allies we have formed a connection with from the
heart. If that connection isn't there, we cannot energet-
ically receive its loving medicine. Notice the plants that
surround you where you are, and which ones you feel a
strong pull toward. Those are your medicine. Cedar and

rosemary are two close allies of mine, but they may not offer you the same healing as they do for me. These simple space clearing rituals can be done with any plant— from the dandelion that grows up from the sidewalk to the pine needles that fall in your neighborhood. Simply create space to commune, connect to the energy of the plant, and set your intention.

◇ **Saltwater.** Salt is also a powerful energy clearer, which is why bathing in salt water, whether in the bath or the ocean, can shift and clear out whatever energies we intend it to. I take a salt bath almost daily to clear out the energy from the day and to create space for my emotional and intuitive energy to flow with more ease. I also keep a shell filled with sea salt or pink salt in all my sacred places to act as an energy clearer for my space so that the energetic waters of my life may flow more freely.

◇ **Breath.** Dropping into your body and connecting to intentional breathing is a beautiful, simple way to clear out any stuck energy. Breath is life force energy—a healing tool at the root of most all ancient healing practices. Taking even three deep breaths when feeling overwhelmed or off-balanced can connect us back to our sacred center.

◇ **Movement.** Moving my body is my go-to ritual practice to transform and express stuck energy and create more space in my body for its natural wisdom and grounded presence. My movement practice is intuitive dancing (sometimes slow and curving with tears streaming down my face, sometimes more passionately to Beyoncé), but whatever feels best and most natural and intuitive for your body will be a healing ally in your journey. Whenever you feel anxiety, tension, fear, or stagnant emotion in your body—aches and pains around the back of your heart, chest, hips, and shoulders/neck (the areas where we tend to hold the most tension)—connect to your body and move it in whatever way feels best.

◇ **Sound.** Sound is the most powerful energy clearer. For me, singing clears out any energy that I am holding onto in my heart and throat. Singing knocks down the walls around my love and opens my heart to grace, and allows me to more easily express myself. I also use musical instruments in my self-tending and client practice to clear energy: a small lyre harp my partner made for me, a flute, drums, rattles, shakers, and singing bowls. I look to sound and music as my ally to open my heart and channels, clear unwanted energies in my auric field, and fortify my boundary of sacred love. You may find that certain music shifts your energy or that having a wind chime outside your front door clears energy in your space. You may find healing in chanting, mantras, humming, or birdsong. Listen and connect to the sounds that create the most space for you.

◇ **Removing distractions.** Distractions can manifest as negative habits, other people's opinions, devices, social media, etc. Distractions carry energy that is not our own and can

prevent us from seeing through the lens of our own truth and love. Simply identifying distractions can create a subtle shift in our reality, giving us space to clear them. When going into a healing ritual, I will often place my phone in another room or clear out distracting thoughts and to-do lists with writing beforehand.

Altars

One way to create space for ritual is to make your own altar. Altars have been around since ancient times for various spiritual reasons. They have been places of worship, connection to Spirit, the self, as well as spaces to offer our gratitude and energy to the Sacred. An altar not only grounds our intention for spiritual work, it also creates a clear energy and acts as an available container for what we are creating. Your altar is an extension of you, your practice, and your connection with the Sacred. You can think about what you put on your altar as a reflection for what you are calling in through your ritual practice. I like a low table for an altar so that I can sit on the ground in front of it, but altars come in any shape, size, color, and material. Your altar could be a fireplace mantle, a windowsill, a shelf, or simply a tree stump outside in your backyard, or even the ground you sit upon.

When creating this sacred space, be mindful of the items you keep at your altar. There are no rules, but the items you choose should be important and feel sacred to you. Create an altar that inspires peace, love, and presence, or anything else you wish to call into your life. You may want to include a photo of something you love most in the world, or a photo of an ancestor, a candle colored in your favorite hue, your favorite flower, a god or goddess figure that inspires you, and tools for your practice—herbs, bells, incense, a journal, feathers, shells, stones, cards, or even this book. Some items I use include beeswax candles, the body of a bee I came across on the ground outside my studio one day, my favorite crystal ally at the moment, a found feather, a couple of little animal ally statues, art depicting allies and guides, fresh flowers, a bowl of water, honey offerings to Spirit, little books of poetry or tarot/oracle cards, a flower essence or tincture I am working with, and a shell filled with pink salt. Bringing the elements and my Earth allies through on my altar reminds me of the connection between all things on Earth and how the elements also move through me (we'll talk more about the elements in the next chapter).

If you don't have space for an altar in your home, you can use yourself as an altar, for that is what you are: a temple for the Sacred. How you adorn your temple creates an intentional ener-gy for your spiritual work. For example, when connecting to ritual you may desire to wear something that inspires you, makes you feel good, and helps you to recognize your divine beauty. You may desire to wear a piece of jewelry that belonged to a family member to feel more connected to their energy and love. You may want to dress in red because it makes you feel more powerful, or yellow because it makes you feel bright. You may think about the stones you wear, the colors and patterns of your clothing, and even how you keep your hair as you practice. Everything from the fabric we put on our bod-ies to the color of our clothing influences our energy and the space we create and take up, for everything is energy.

You don't need to buy anything extra for this practice, just allow yourself to become more intentional. Each day I like to dress to align with what I am calling in for the day. On days I feel like I need to tend to my inner child, I wear something bright and playful that inspires freedom and creativity, along with a necklace from my youth. On days where I feel like I need to rest and heal, I wear my comfiest clothing to feel warm and nourished, as well as grounding oils. On days I spend writing, I often wear green or blue, with pearls or blue stones. Treating the body like an altar and intentionally adorning it is my favorite way to create space every day because it connects me to the beauty and sacredness of my physical form and how I wish to express myself through it. It is a practice I learned from my grandmother that grew over time as I noticed how my energy shifted when I adorned my temple in new ways that spoke to me.

Most of all, remember to breathe. Your sacred breath creates the most space of all.

Love

At the deepest root of your practice is the energy of love. This is the fuel for all that you do in your sacred tending. There isn't a more beautiful part of the human experience than exploring the depths of love. We are all expansive, beautiful beings of love—a love that cannot be found outside of ourselves, a love that never loses its way, a love unwavering in all its divine devotion. We are created from love and are all here to return to its pure, loving essence. Commitment to our love is what carries us toward our inner desires and truth. Your ritual practice is the bridge that connects you to your love, guiding you to be in flow with life and its loving rhythms.

Our hearts are our gifts and their potential is beyond logical understanding. All spiritual work asks us to have an open heart and to commit to softening and opening more and more as we grow. It is through this openness that we find the Sacred within and bear witness to our infinite love. Life in all its chaos and struggle often makes us shut down and put up walls around our hearts to feel safe and in control. We are so afraid of rejection, change, and being unworthy that we become so good at hiding from love, forgetting that love is our key to freedom. We so easily close off and let fear, ego, and shadow run the show, creating false storylines and blocking the energy of love. This not only keeps us from receiving all the love that wishes to enter our lives, but also disconnects us from our own love and the power of our sacred hearts. Fear and love cannot coexist.

Though emotion is the most powerful part of the human experience, it is also the most misunderstood and dismissed. Collectively we have been conditioned for centuries to not fully express this holy power and to not be in tune with the expression of love from within. We so often close off any emoting, especially in public, because it's too much, too messy, or too hard to handle. We may even receive messages telling us that what we feel is crazy or that we are being hysterical. For thousands of years, hysteria was a disease invented by men to pathologize the natural waves of feminine emotion, creating even more conditioning and fear around our emotional

expression. This discouraged generation after generation of women to channel emotions in healthy ways and created blockages in receiving from our hearts. Doing this causes most of our physical, emotional, and mental imbalances, which we will explore in the next chapter. Even today, we live in a society with low emotional intelligence that values work over pleasure and is fueled by fear over love. And as a result, we are collectively, seriously, and emotionally repressed. This keeps us from truly connecting to and receiving all the love that is available. Our greatest spiritual challenge in this life is to become open and embrace love. We must break open our hearts in order to feel the Sacred. This is sacred tending at its deepest level.

In order to open our hearts, we must learn to become receptive. Beyond emotion and love not being modeled, celebrated, and expressed in healthy ways in our society, far too many of us don't receive love as a child from others or don't know how to receive love from ourselves. This can be a challenging—though life-changing—lesson to learn on our spiritual paths. Most of us are taught through societal and familial programming that receiving is selfish or that it is not safe. Deep within, we may feel that we are unworthy, undeserving, or not capable of receiving love. That we are unlovable. This may create patterns of codependency, avoiding love, and even depression.

Receptivity to love requires a sacred pause and intentional presence to our hearts. When was the last time you really allowed yourself to be receptive of your emotions, to give them space and attention to be heard and felt without shame or control? When was the last time you paused to receive the beauty of nature in your heart? When was the last time you listened to and followed your heart, even though your mind was leading you elsewhere, clouding you with logic and reason? Or allowed yourself to truly receive love from another, even in the form of a loving compliment—not brushing it off, but feeling the compliment fully in your heart? We learn this lesson of receiving by moving toward the challenges that ask us to let go and surrender to love, in moving closer to those who love us, letting our walls down, being vulnerable, and by softening, little by little. Letting in the energy of pure love is the sole energy responsible for completely changing our lives. It is the energy you will unlock through your ritualistic tending.

Emotions are pure energy in motion. They let us know what is/is not working, help us to process life and all its complexities, guide us home to our hearts, and help us grow and evolve. They are not static and cannot be contained in a box, labeled, or stuffed away in hopes that they will disappear. Our hearts beat strong for us, carrying us through grief, sorrow, pain, joy, and pleasure without ever needing to be conscious of their sacred rhythms. This is pure divine nature. We can only love as much as we learn to open, grieve, and feel. All emotions, even the most painful, carry powerful lessons, truth, and blessings. This is why the opening of our hearts is an essential part of our ritual work. When we are closed off from the flow of our hearts, emotional energy gets stuck in our bodies and manifests in various physical ways, keeping us further and further away from our truth and our love. As we collectively begin to lift the gates of repression and let out waves of pain, grief, frustration, shame, and anger, and open to the fullness of love, we must learn how to hold space to let the emotions flow. The more we open our hearts—the more space we create for joy, love, purpose, and the Sacred—the more connected to love all around we become. Open your heart and revel in the power you find.

RITUAL TO OPEN TO LOVE

If you are feeling closed off from love, from your emotions, from your spiritual practice, or from receiving, this is a beautiful, simple ritual to open your heart and connect back to its loving essence. You can use this practice at the start of any ritual to guide you to whatever intention you need today, to move energy to create more internal space, or simply to connect to the energy of love for the day.

At your altar, outside in your favorite place in nature, in bed, a bath, or simply in a comfy seated position, connect to your breath. Take six slow counts in, and six counts out. Do this for a few moments as you find presence and connection to your body, allowing your mind to soften and your focus to come into the heart. Notice in your body where you may be holding onto any emotional tension. Maybe it's tension in your neck and shoulders, hips, or tenderness in your heart. Breathe into that space for a few breaths, allowing your breath to begin to loosen the energy.

Now, bring your attention and breath to your heart space. Imagine your heart filling up with a green light with each inhale and any tension melting like honey, dripping down and back into the Earth with each exhale. Place your hands on your heart and continue with deep breaths. Let yourself feel whatever emotions are wanting to move from your body. You may feel the need to cry, yell, scream, laugh, smile, or sing. You may feel confused, frustrated, happy, sad, disappointed, grateful, encouraged, ashamed, excited, etc. Whatever emotion arises, give it space. Remember, tears cleanse the Spirit. It is the most powerful healing you can receive. Don't create a story around the emotion however it arises. You don't need to know where it came from, who or what caused it, or feel shame for expressing it. It could be something you picked up during the week, something from ten years ago, or even an energy you carried through your ancestral lineage. Its origin does not matter. All that matters right now is the movement of the emotion—letting it out in whatever way it needs to. If you have trouble expressing the emotion, try giving it a sound and making the sound as a way to move it out of your body. Movement can also help, or any of the tools for space clearing discussed before. Take as long or as short as you need to move the emotion.

   To uplift and protect your open heart, imagine a golden orb of light surrounding you and slowly moving through your body, into your heart, and glowing outwards, cleansing your energy. When you feel complete,

> give yourself a hug, a squeeze, or a little self-massage
> in those spaces holding tension. Allow yourself to be
> open to your love. Journal any discoveries, visions,
> feelings, or insights.

It is our love that forms new patterns, new awarenesses, and new ways of being. With each powerful opening, connection to love, and emotional release, our heart opens a little wider to the spiritual love that is available all around us. With love, all is possible.

Belief

Our beliefs are at the very root of our reality. What we believe is what we create and witness in our lives. If we don't believe in love, we will never find it. If we don't believe it is possible to be successful in our dream career, we will not align with it. If we don't believe in our power to heal and connect to Spirit, we will be closed off from receiving from Spirit. If we grow up under a specific structure of beliefs, we may not realize that there is another world outside of those beliefs. In tending to the Sacred you must believe in yourself and your power. You must believe you are worthy of growing and evolving. You must believe in your ability to receive love, to change your reality, to create, to move energy, to connect to your truth and your soul's purpose, and most of all, connect to the Sacred.

When we boil it down, belief relies on the energy of trust. To form our own beliefs outside of the norm of what we were told or shown on our paths, we must have radical self-trust. To believe in our spiritual evolution and our ability to co-create with the Universe, we must trust in the Universe—in the unknown and the unseen. To believe we can receive love, we must trust love. Trust is the energy that allows us to receive. It allows us to see what is true and moves us into alignment.

We first learn trust in infancy—a time when we are completely codependent on others, fully relying on our caretakers for our basic needs to be met. If those core needs aren't taken care of, we often don't learn to trust others, and that belief that we can't rely on others to get our basic needs met gets imprinted within. This often programs the belief that we are on our own separate journeys, separate from Spirit and all its divine support.

We must look back into our childhoods to find the root of our distrust. Where we originally learn that it isn't safe to trust creates an ongoing pattern in our lives that mirrors that distrust, keeping us further and further away from receiving and trusting in love. Lack of trust typically translates into a feeling of needing to be in full control. When we have a need to be in control, it is difficult to trust in the mysterious power of the Universe and all its magic. When we need to be in control, it can be hard to believe that anyone can help us, keeping love and intimacy with life at a distance. To tend to the Sacred it's important to believe that we can control the destiny of our lives and call forth our dreams, while also receiving the love, support, and divine assistance to help make our dreams a reality. We are not here to do anything alone. We must trust in the interconnectedness of all. We must trust that

Spirit is listening to our intentions. We must trust, with our open hearts, that the Universe is always supporting us and tending to us. We must trust that our souls chose this body, this time, this life for our soul's evolution. And in order to trust all of the above, we must most of all trust ourselves and trust our desires. Trusting yourself is a sacred act of divinity.

RITUAL FOR REMOVING LIMITING BELIEFS

With the intention of liberation, make a list in your journal of all the limiting beliefs you've inherited along your path—any belief that holds you back from living out your wildest, most abundant dreams and loving truth. A limiting belief is any lie you told yourself or were told—any belief that says you are unworthy or not good enough (especially any beliefs that begin with the words "I shouldn't," or "I can't"). It may help to meditate or do the Love Ritual practice before you do this, to awaken your heart and subconscious mind (where the limits are rooted). These beliefs will be what you return to again and again in your healing ritual practice to see where your mental energy blocks are held. Some examples include:

◇ *"I believe I am unworthy of love or success,
because I wasn't accepted for who I am by my
parents."*

◇ *"I believe I am not beautiful, because I don't match
the idea of beauty portrayed and celebrated in the
media and society."*

◇ *"I believe I have to do everything on my own, because I couldn't trust anyone to help me as a child."*

◇ *"I believe in facts and evidence, because it is the
only way my knowledge and opinions will be
valued and taken seriously."*

◇ *"I believe I am not valuable and cannot achieve
my dreams, because it has never been done before by a person like me."*

Some emotions may come up for you when journaling out your limiting beliefs. Allow all emotions to
flow out of your being and dissolve away.

Next, identify the age in which you inherited these
beliefs, from any specific memories that have sur-
faced. Write out specific memories in which you felt
these beliefs form. A personal example: when I was
young my mother (jokingly) once told me I wouldn't

get married or find someone to love, which mani-
fested as a strong belief that I would never find love
and have a long-term partnership, until I cleared
this limiting belief. When we are young we do not
consciously understand subtleties of language and
tone. We instead understand things in extremes.
If someone says "you can't do that," we take it to
heart—even if they are not being serious—and we
place that belief where we carry our wounds.

Visualize that version of yourself and give them
the love and support they need to believe in what is
true in their hearts—a hug, a healing talk, encouragement, acceptance, and comfort. Maybe they need
play to remind them that life is joyful, maybe they
just need to sing. Listen to the music that version of
you once loved to dance to, eat your favorite food
from that age, call up a best friend from that time,
revisit your favorite activities, or simply tell yourself
the things you needed to hear at that age. Giving
versions of yourself that are holding onto old and
limiting beliefs the love and support they desire
tends to the wounds they still carry.

This is a beautiful ritual practice to free ourselves
to connect to the Sacred. I find this practice to be
effective anytime something is triggering, a wound
resurfaces, or I feel frustrated about something I
desire. Repeat this process anytime a limiting belief

surfaces that stops you from moving forward on your path or connecting to your essence of sacred love within.

If love and intention are the fuel of ritual, beliefs are the wheel. They dictate where your sacred ship is heading in your practice. Your ritual practice relies on your beliefs being expanded in order to have direction toward the Sacred love that is guiding you home. Everything in our reality can change just from this practice alone. We need to free ourselves to believe anything is possible in order to live a life full of love, grace, purpose, and freedom from all that holds us back.

Chapter Two

Understanding Energy

Everything is energy. You are energy, this book is energy, your food is energy, as are your words, movements, the clouds, colors, symbols, objects, and plants. Everything beyond this material planet is also energy. Everything in the Universe has its own unique energetic vibration. We usually complicate the understanding of energy by trying to define it logically or find evidence to support it in all its multidimensionality. But energy is not something we can understand with just the mind or see with the naked eye, it must be viewed through the lenses we gain on our spiritual journeys. With the spiritual eye of observation we may witness all the infinite realms of energy that swirl around in a marvelous dance of the unseen.

We are taught in grade school that energy can neither be created nor destroyed, but that it can be altered. Energy can be stagnant or flowing, slowed down or sped up, controlled or released, and transformed. Before going any further, it's important to note that there is no such thing as good and bad energy. There is only energy that lies on a spectrum of light and dark, but these dualities are necessary energies that make up the balance of existence, walking side by side in harmony when in balance—within and without. We cannot have light without the dark. You can also think of these energies as fueled by fear or fueled by love. What we perceive as dark or negative energy is simply the lack of a conscious awareness of love. When we bring loving awareness to whatever we perceive as dark, the energy moves.

As I mentioned in the Space portion in the previous chapter, everything in our lives has a vibrational effect on our energy. Certain foods can deplete our energy, as can certain people, words, sounds, situations, beliefs not authentic to our soul's truth, and repressed or stuck emotions. Too much depleted energy can cause our physical systems to live in a state of poor energy and poor health. Alternatively, when our intention and consciousness is directed toward creation, freedom, love, and healing, we raise our vibration and align with things, people, and situations that match that vibration. To truly understand and feel energy, we must get quiet and attune ourselves to the subtle vibrations around us and observe the cause and effect. For example, cultivating presence through ritual work may make our energy grounded and balanced. When we eat something our body doesn't register as healthy, our energy may manifest in a low, poor state. When we allow tears to flow freely, we may feel a release of energy from our bodies and experience more ease and calm, or even feel depleted afterward as the loss of emotional energy clears space from our being (at which point I recommend filling your energy back up with nourishing things).

Throughout your journey in this book you can always connect to your energy at the moment by closing your eyes and connecting to the subtle vibration within and around you, noticing your body, breath, feelings, tension, the sounds and movement around you, your intuition and desires. Just observe.

Types of Energy

◇ **Universal or spiritual.** The sacred unseen. The life force energy of creation and loving mystery. When we attune to the Sacred and place our trust in the Universe, this energy flows. When we feel separate, think of ourselves as the victim of our own lives, lack faith in our journeys, or force our paths, this energy becomes blocked. I experienced a blocked flow of universal energy when I completely cut myself off from the Sacred (as I mentioned in the introduction, right before my meeting with the bee spirit). At that point in my life, it felt like the Universe was intentionally making my life a living hell and I lost all trust in myself, my relationships, and Spirit. To unblock this energy and move into a state of flow, I had to take control of my life and begin co-creating with the Universe from a space of trust, and establish a loving relationship, thereby letting Spirit know I was ready to honor my truth. Ritual has always been the bridge that creates a flow of spiritual energy in my life.

When this energy flows, the Universe lovingly responds to our desires, wishes, and struggles. We move into alignment. When this energy flows, it does not mean that everything in life is sunshine and rainbows and spiritually enlightened. It means you are in total alignment on your spiritual path, which will include some challenging moments of learning to evolve, but also moments of blessings, and all fueled by this energy of universal love.

◇ **Emotional.** Feelings and moods. Emotional energetic blocks are the root of most imbalances in our modern times. This is because we are repressed from allowing the free flow of energy from our hearts as mentioned in the Love section in the previous chapter. We can slowly begin to heal our emotional blocks by being vulnerable and openhearted, healing fears, and tending to our wounding and trauma. When I experience blocked emotions, it almost immediately manifests physically with anxiety, pain, or sometimes illness. I tend to these blocks by being present with what they are trying to tell me, listening to my body and heart, and connecting to my ritual tools to assist the energy in moving. While we don't need to create a story around our emotional energy to heal it, understanding the root energy of each emotion can often help us to release it, to heal, and to open up more fully to the energy of love within us. I will delve into this more later in the chapter.

◇ **Physical.** Body and Earth. What is tangible. When we are disconnected from the wisdom and needs of our bodies—

that is, when we're not in a healthy, loving relationship with our bodies—this energy is blocked. It is also blocked whenever we live in a fear of scarcity, feel unsupported or disconnected from the Earth (for example, we see ourselves are separate from the Earth), and focus too much on the material world from a space of lack (money, jobs, material goods, and so on). This energy flows when we attune to the natural rhythms of our bodies and the Earth, treat both with love and respect, and have a healthy relationship with money and the material realm. When living in New York City, this was a significant block I worked through with myself and a number of clients and friends. With the lack of nature, abundance of lights and stimulants, all the people and hustle, and the stress around money and work, I found that the collective energy lacks the grounding presence that physical energy provides. What helps this energy flow freely is simply prioritizing grounding, which we will get into much more in the next chapter.

◇ **Mental.** Consciousness, subconscious beliefs, and thoughts. When our minds are closed off and our belief system is fixed—seeing things in absolutes, unable to expand into new awareness or beyond the realms of rigid thinking—this energy is blocked. This energy is also out of balance when we spend too much time in our minds and aren't present. When we are open mentally, are consciously aware of our thoughts and beliefs, and free ourselves with sacred tending to expand our consciousness, this energy flows. We can heal mental energetic blocks by recognizing our thoughts

as energy and noticing where our thinking is rigid or linear. Conservative religion and political parties are examples of repressed mental energy. They approach things in absolutes and are one-sided, seeing one truth as *the* truth, viewing one way as *the* way, following set rules and structures laid out by the mind. The ritual in the last chapter in the Belief section is helpful in releasing these types of mental energetic blocks.

◇ **Psychic.** Subtle energetic awareness of life. Energetic bridge that connects us to the universal. Also known as intuition and psychic wisdom. Mental, spiritual, or emotional obstacles can all block us from our psychic energy. Every single person on this planet is psychic or intuitive. This is not energy reserved for those special few born with magical gifts and powers. We are all magical and powerful with the ability to access this energy. We only need to unblock the flow of our repressed energy and open to our intuitive energy—our inner well of deep wisdom. When clients tell me they feel blocked from their intuition and want to learn to connect to this energy, my first response is to ask, "Are you listening?" When we are blocked mentally with outdated ways of thinking—even the beliefs that we are not intuitive enough, that we are not capable of tending to our inner selves, or we are ignoring our needs, or not connecting to the Sacred—then we will not witness the expansive and powerful flow of our inner wisdom. The easiest way to allow this energy to flow is to become quiet and listen. It is an ongoing practice, and one that ritual so beautifully assists with. I will share a ritual for connecting to intuition in chapter eight.

All these energies exist within and around us at all times. Energetic blocks occur through a lack of awareness, a lack of love, and a lack of attention. Understanding and altering energy is not only healing for ourselves, but for our whole planet. We must collectively take responsibility for the way we consume, change, share, take in, and fix energy to create a harmonious flow of energy in our lives and on our Earth. As you journey into the energetics of ritual guided by the four pillars I mentioned before, you will begin to become more aware of your own energy, notice how it responds to life, discern what serves your energy and what does not, and understand how to use it in a conscious and loving way, appreciating all the energies that flow in and out of your sacred being.

Understanding Emotional Energy

Suppressed emotional energy takes on many forms, but tending to emotional energy allows us to heal and walk forward on our paths with more ease and resilience. What we resist persists. This is why this part of your tending is the most important for creating change in your life. The guide below may assist you in working with your emotional energy as it comes up as you journey into sacred tending. Though this list is what I connect to with my own intuitive wisdom and use with my clients, I encourage you to make your own list of different emotions and what they are associated with. It may help to identify the source of the emotion from memory. For example, if you harbor lasting anger toward a parent who didn't give you the love and attention you needed when you were a child, you may have anger triggered when you feel you are not being seen, heard, or loved in the way you need by another person, even by yourself. Knowing this can help heal this emotion by giving yourself the love you so strongly desire. Explore your relationship with all your various feelings. Name your emotion and let it guide you in ritual. Explore where you feel it in your body. Feel your emotions fully, for that is the only way to clear your emotional energy. Cherish all your pain and emotions as sacred teachers. Emotional pain is not in itself bad, and it is safe to feel fully. Your emotions are all guiding you toward love.

Where there is energetic stagnation in the body, there is often physical pain, tension, or ailments. These pains can be chronic, flare up when experiencing certain emotions, or get triggered by a particular experience or energetic release. For example, when I am worrying too much about my partner, clients, or others (for example, wanting to help and "fix" them), I feel a rock solid tension in my shoulders. This worry is not in alignment with my truth, but it is a sacred teacher. Whenever it surfaces, it is my body's way of saying, "Hey, something needs to shift." I then know I need to let go and allow others to process through their own journey in their own way, that it is not my responsibility to do the work for them. I can then take this energy through a ritual to shift me back into my own energy, such as the Letting Go Ritual you'll learn in chapter eighteen.

The table below can help navigate how energy can show up in your body. Our bodies are powerful guides in our healing journey. Everything that manifests physically is a symbol for your healing.

EMOTION ROOT

Anger — WHERE OUR BOUNDARIES HAVE BEEN CROSSED. LACK OF BOUNDARIES OR NEEDS BEING MET

Sadness — THE DEPTHS OF OUR FEELINGS

Shame — INTERNALIZING CONDITIONINGS, JUDGMENTS AND PROJECTIONS FROM OTHERS

Guilt — LIVING IN OTHERS BELIEFS OR EXPECTATIONS

Jealousy/Envy — NOT IN POWER. PROJECTING LACK OR DOUBT ONTO OTHERS. WITNESSING WHAT YOU DESIRE

Resentment — ATTACHMENTS TO THE PAST. STUCK EMOTIONS. GRUDGES

Frustration — NOT LISTENING TO NEEDS OR DESIRES

Anxiety — NOT IN THE PRESENT. NOT HOLDING SPACE FOR EMOTIONAL ENERGY

Bitterness — JUDGMENT OR DEEP CRITCISM TOWARD SELF

RESISTANCE & EMOTIONS FELT IN THE BODY

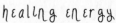

body placement	emotion	healing energy
Stomach	Worry, anxiety, not listening to gut desires	Surrender and self-trust
Liver	Anger, frustration, resentment, toxic will	Surrender and forgiveness
Lungs	Grief	Allowance and patience
Heart	Despair, depression, hate, impatience	Presence and love
Kidneys/Adrenals	Fear, anxiety	Love, trust and presence
Lower Back Pain	Fear of scarcity, primal security fears	Self-security, letting go of control
Upper Back Pain	Fear of love/receiving, afraid to trust, lack of presence and gratitude	Trust and love
Neck Pain	Fear of expression, fear of trusting others/ judgment fears	Trust, courage, and vulnerability
Knee Pain	Ego fears/ fear of change	Courage and faith
Hip Pain	Fear of expansion, fear of creation (life/death)	Passion, creative expression, and freedom
Wrist Pain	Fear of losing control, fear of being flexible and flowing with life	Trust and flow
Ankle Pain	Fear of weakness, lack of boundaries	Acceptance and self-love
Shoulder Pain	Fear for others, fear of responsibility, holding weight of the world	Letting go of pressure, and worry for others, self-focus, ask for help.

Emotional Triggers

An emotional trigger occurs when something happens or someone says something that brings up a past emotion stored within. We often see the phrase *trigger warning* attached to stories and media in which trauma is discussed, but triggers can be found anywhere—in our interactions with others, while scrolling social media, walking down the street, in the news, in our family dynamics, in our own habits and thought patterns, and elsewhere. A personal example: When proofreading the first draft of this book with my partner, the first person I let read my entire manuscript, he gave me some constructive criticism that was at first hard to digest. At first I got defensive and angry, then quite emotional with tears. This was a huge, unexpected emotional trigger, even though he meant no harm and gave me much more beautiful, loving feedback than critical notes. But for my heart, it felt so heavy to receive in that moment, as this trigger was wanting to move energy from my being and create healing around the wound it came from.

Criticism was something I endured chronically in my youth from my mother, not to mention the criticism the feminine voice has received for far longer. Because of my mother's own unmet needs, conditioning, and wounding, she criticized every sound that came out of my mouth, how I styled my hair, my inner and outer qualities, and every self-expression outlet I had from as young as I can remember, causing much fear around my expression. Because of these stuck emotions in my body, when someone I love and trust criticized a way I express myself, I was transported back to those emotions of my youth. The anger I felt was old, the defensiveness was my form of protection I learned from that period of my life, and the tears that followed carried my pain from not feeling like I could be myself and share myself as a child.

When we are triggered emotionally, whether it is fear, anger, or jealousy, these are moments that call us to open our hearts and heal. We must trust their arrival and make space for the healing to flow. The goal is to have the courage to hold space for all our triggers and process through them—even (and most especially) the intense emotional triggers. We must learn to embrace our triggers. Triggers are a gift that teach us where the work needs to be done and can lead us to our intention in our ritual work. Since our triggers are rooted in a space of fear, after we feel through the emotions of a trigger, we must give ourselves love. When a trigger shows up, take it through your ritual practice to hold space for it and heal.

Begin to notice your triggers by noticing when you become defensive, upset over something seemingly minor, or are suddenly shifted into an old, dense emotion. Triggers aren't something we can avoid. I won't completely avoid criticism in this world doing and sharing the work I do until all people are navigating from love instead of fear, and acceptance over judgment. There will still be internet trolls, bullies, envy, judgments, projections, disbelief, and societal programming until everyone begins to radically heal. But even so, through our emotional awareness and ritual practices we begin to lessen the blow and not be affected by them. The more we heal, the more resilient we become, the more we can handle, and the less we are triggered. It was important to work through my criticism trigger when I first wrote this book so that I would be able to emotionally handle any criticism that came after, as I share this book with the world!

Energetic Balance

In order to create balance in our lives, we must create balance within. All energy that exists can be described as *divine feminine* or *divine masculine* (or just feminine and masculine). These terms refer to the energetics of feminine and masculine, but they have very little to do with gender as the words are used as labels today. The divine feminine speaks to love, receptivity, being, allowing, feeling, flow, lunar energy, creation, voice, sensuality, water, earth, intuition, and contraction. These are energies which are seldom celebrated in our current timeline, which is why feminine energy—not just women, but creativity, intuition, sacred tending, emotions, etc.—are repressed in our world. Individually, these feminine energies can be harder to cultivate from within because they are more inward, subtle, unseen, beyond logical understanding, and often shamed for embodying. The divine masculine speaks to consciousness, thinking, mind, action, protection, activation, structure, fire, air, solar energy, doing, ordering, controlling, and expansion. The masculine energies are dominant in our human collective at this time and they are energies we see modeled by our culture and society every day. As a result, they are often easier for us to cultivate.

Neither energy is better or worse. It is only when the balance is knocked off-center, or we navigate only from the shadow aspects of that energy and suffer from the detriments of that. We all contain both the divine feminine and divine masculine within, no matter what physical sex we identify as, but we must learn to find balance within these two core energies as they flow from within. We need both aspects healthy and flowing to be in alignment with our own energy, and for the energy of our world to be in balance. When we find balance with these energies individually, we will begin to see it ripple out into our collective, creating balance all around.

When we are in energetic flow in our lives, we maintain a healthy balance of these energies and they work in partnership with one another. As we are currently living in a harsh patriarchal timeline, most of our individual healing work lies in healing and unleashing our feminine power and restoring feminine balance— the infinite potential of our sacred loving hearts. When we learn to fully embody the feminine—the energy of love—we can heal ourselves and the whole planet. It's important to just check in along your path to make sure you are maintaining a state of balance. The ritual below can help.

INNER BALANCE RITUAL

Balance is important to cultivate for a life of flow. When you are navigating too much from your masculine energy—overthinking, overworking, and pushing ahead with force—practice the feminine rituals to find your balance. If you are navigating from a space of too much feminine, feel stuck in the weight of your emotions, experience the emotional weight of the world, or are unable to ground your intuitive impulses, engage in the masculine activities to bring you back into a state of balance. If you are unsure of which energy you are dominant in, notice where you are most comfortable (thinking or feeling? being or doing?), as well as which energies you lead with. Remember your four pillars of ritual as you connect to the one that feels most aligned.

To Honor Your Masculine Energy

◇ Ground into your body with active movement/exercise

◇ Take action toward a passion burning within by taking more initiative and setting goals (see the Manifestation Ritual, chapter fourteen)

◇ Connect with your inner warrior—the version of self who protects you with courage and strength (Resilience Mist, chapter nineteen)

◇ Commit to a daily grounding ritual practice for forty days (Grounding Ritual, chapter three)

◇ Be assertive and stand your ground with self-respect (Ritual for Boundaries, chapter thirteen)

To Honor Your Feminine Energy

- ◇ Find time for sacred pauses for healing ritual and rest

- ◇ Hold space for your emotions, removing fear around vulnerability (Water Ritual, chapter eight)

- ◇ Meditate and take time for self-care (Self-Care ritual, chapter fifteen)

- ◇ Listen to your intuition (Moon Water, chapter eight)

Chapter Three

Grounding

I n order to embody our truest essence, find purpose and direction, and remain centered through all of life's challenges and cycles, we must find our solid ground. Our inner foundation is the anchor that keeps us focused and steady on our spiritual paths. To be fully anchored in the body on this Earth, it is important to feel comfortable in the body and attuned to how it responds to life, and always acknowledge our relationship with the ground we stand on. To ground is to feel life fully—all the emotions of our human experiences, moving through life in a state of flow that opens us up to all that is sacred.

The first step to getting rooted in our bodies is healing the nervous system through recognizing and healing our traumas. All humans have experienced trauma, whether it is systemic, ancestral, familiar, or from a specific event or physical trauma. Even being born can be a trauma for sensitive spirits. Most of us experience traumatic situations everyday with the news triggering fear, advertisements triggering shame, and endless war of varying degrees triggering trauma responses in the body. Traumatic experiences can take the form of huge life-altering events or even experiences we don't register as trauma because they're considered normal—getting bullied on the playground as a seven-year-old, being verbally put down by a parent for getting a B- instead of an A in school, being told we're not good enough to play the piano or sing, getting into a car accident, suffering assault or abuse, or experiencing anything in which we feel shame or fear.

Our bodies carry our traumas, not our minds. To survive, we mentally compartmentalize and control our emotional responses to feel safe, but this leads to feeling unsafe or insecure in our bodies, which in turn leads us to navigating life slightly outside of our bodies, disconnected from their innate wisdom. Our bodies store the traumatic emotional memory within until we decide to feel and heal it. If we are afraid of our emotions because of a past trauma, we will naturally disconnect from our bodies and this process will be harder. This manifests most often within the nervous system as anxiety as we are unable to root in the now and be fully present in our bodies. Without even realizing, we are subtly replaying the response our bodies had to our traumas any time even mild stress is triggered in the body. This stress, when held in the body without release, creates tension, ailments, imbalances, even disease.

Until I began healing my nervous system, whenever I felt even the slightest bit stressed or overwhelmed in my life, my body's natural posture would retreat into a sort of half fetal position. My shoulders would raise and round, my neck would move forward, I would get tense, and even experience severe pain at times, from the top of my spine to the middle of my back. This is my body's learned response to stress—my programmed fight-or-flight reaction from trauma I experienced in my youth. You see this type of response in animals—for example, when your pet hears a new noise. Your dog may instantly bark and growl and go into fight mode, and your cat may cower or jump and run and hide in order to flee. This is what they learned to protect themselves.

Unlike animals, we don't naturally follow our instincts to release the stress from our bodies, because collectively, we don't prioritize self-care. Most people just don't have the tools they need to heal. The back of my heart is the main space where I have held the tension of my trauma from my youth, so if stress gets triggered in my body, that part of my body closes off and creates a shell of protection. It is my little/big trauma backpack. My body learned this response to stress to keep me safe as a child—to close off my heart from receiving because it was not safe to be open and sensitive, which served me at the time. But this also meant that I lived most of my life disconnected from my body and heart until I decided to heal down to the root of that learned response and began to emotionally release the initial traumas from my body through my healing ritual practices. This is groundwork at its deepest level. This part of my healing is what changed everything for me and allowed me to live a life with more presence, joyful embodiment, ease, and grace. Without this healing, grounding and showing up confident and present in my body would not be possible for me.

As a highly sensitive woman who channels, communes with Spirit, and practices healing work, grounding is my most beloved daily, absolutely mandatory, ritual practice. For all sensitive beings, regardless of trauma, prioritizing grounding is a must upon waking from the dream state each morning. The practice of grounding on a path of healing is truly one of the greatest tools we can cultivate. It reminds us that we are here, we are safe, and we are present—engaged with life and supported by the body and the Earth that carries us.

Along with life in general and all the trauma any given person can endure, the path of tending to the Sacred can be a little overwhelming in the beginning. Our spiritual awakenings to new awarenesses and healing releases can lead to periods of confusion, anxiety, heightened sensitivity, spiritual crisis, emotional overwhelm, huge expansion and radical life shifts, and sometimes even illness and painful contractions as we release old stuck energies. All of these energies serve our evolution, but it is important to learn to work with them. The new awarenesses we gain on our spiritual paths surrounding energy, Spirit, intuition, and so on take our energy upward to the mind as we learn and begin to see through our spiritual lenses, creating both expansion and release of mental and psychic energy in the head. When we try to understand our spiritual transformations with just our minds—not our inner knowing and our hearts—it will be much harder to embody the changes we are making. We can find ourselves living more in our heads than our bodies, especially if that is our natural default from our traumatic experiences we carry in our bodies or our conditioning. But the more we expand our awarenesses and evolve on our paths, the more we must ground down and anchor into our bodies on this Earth.

When I birthed my Soul Tattoo® practice and started one-on-one healing work full time, my expansion was wildly expedited because I had courageously stepped into alignment with purpose by being of service. So much was shifting and happening in all areas of my life. It was the first year of business, I had just met my life partner, fell in love, moved across the country from New York City to San Francisco, and accumulated a clientele waitlist of more than seven years (less than a year after starting the business). I felt overwhelmed by all of it—my gratitude, the stress, shock, change, the long hours, new awarenesses, the sensitivities and gifts that were newly emerging, so many new people in my life, and everything in between. Looking back, I think I must have gotten through that first year on pure adrenaline, but it was my practice of grounding into my body and my heart that helped me stay fortified, focused, and committed to love.

In order to remain balanced and to remember our purpose, intention, and physical reality, we must practice grounding rituals to return to ourselves, the Earth, and our bodies as a cornerstone of our sacred tending practice. When we are ungrounded, we are unfocused, easily distracted, anxious, disconnected from feeling pleasure, and it is harder to put our new awarenesses into action in our lives. The practice of grounding is to bring our energy back down into our bodies and the Earth, creating roots that anchor us in this physical reality. When you are grounded, you are present and rooted in your being, as well as connected to the essence of who you are and how you are authentically aligned to show up in the world. A daily grounding ritual can strengthen intuition, maintain healthy boundaries, fortify the aura, balance emotional energy, promote clarity, build confidence, reduce stress and anxiety, help you sleep, boost motivation, affirm your purpose and truth, and even cultivate better posture as you stand more rooted in yourself. If there is just one ritual you take away from your journey through this book, let it be this.

GROUNDING RITUAL

Begin your ritual either standing or sitting with your feet flat on the floor. Set your intention to ground and anchor fully into your body on the Earth. You can light incense or a plant ally at this time if you wish. Take deep breaths in a series of four counts (inhale for four, exhale for four, and repeat four times) with one hand on your heart and one on your lap. When you are finished with this breathing practice, just breathe softly and naturally and attune yourself to the ground and your body. You may do this by noticing the sounds, subtle movements, colors, temperature, and smells of the day. Notice how your body feels and just be present with what arises. Next, imagine roots coming down from your feet and slowly moving deep and spreading wide beneath the Earth. Allow these roots to bring your energy down into the Earth. Now, imagine that rich, dark green energy from the Earth is flowing up from your roots and slowing making its way into your feet, legs, and hips. Allow this Earth energy to ground and nourish you, feeling and breathing into it for as long as it takes until the image is clear. You may wish to repeat the visualization process a few times until you are feeling fully anchored and present. This five to ten minute ritual can be done any time you feel ungrounded throughout your days.

Other Ways to Ground Your Energy

◇ Go out in nature and place your bare feet, hands, or body on the Earth. Place your feet or hands on tree roots

◇ Practice slow, deep breathing

◇ Take a break from stimulants (caffeine, screens, etc.)

◇ Go for a walk in nature and connect to the elements (Ritual to Connect to the Elements, chapter four)

◇ Connect to animals or children

◇ Garden

◇ Go for a run or move your body in whatever way feels best

◇ Eat grounding foods such as root vegetables, lentils, and healthy fats

⬦ Work with grounding herbal allies (Grounding Herbal Infusions, immediately below)

Grounding Herbal Infusions

These herbal infusions are my go-to when I need grounding support. All these plants are *nervines*, meaning they support the nervous system and are beautifully relaxing allies. You should be able to find all of these herbs at your local apothecary or even your grocery store, though many are easy enough to grow on your own if you have the space! Add these soothing drinks to any of your grounding rituals for more support in your tending to the Sacred.

Daytime Grounding Infusion Recipe

⬦ In a mason jar, tea pot, or French press, combine 1 heaping tablespoon milky oat tops, 1 heaping tablespoon chamomile, and 1 heaping tablespoon lemon balm.

⬦ Top with recently boiled water and steep for at least 45 minutes and up to 8 hours. If using a mason jar, be sure to strain the herbs out, but otherwise pour and enjoy. Sip slowly and mindfully throughout the day. You can also let the infusion cool naturally for at least 30 minutes, then further steep it in the fridge for a few hours before serving, or pour over ice.

⬦ Oat is one of my favorite plant allies for nervous system nourishment. As one of the oldest plants our species has consumed, it feels so grounding and calming, supporting the nervous system and combating daily stress. This ally is also helpful when stress causes fatigue and burnout from being overworked. When I am working a lot, I sip oatstraw, oat tops, eat lots of oatmeal, and even lie in tall oat grasses if they are present.

◇ Chamomile is a soft but mighty herbal ally, used since ancient times all over the world. It is beautifully calming and soothing to mental stress. It also unwinds nervous tension held in our bellies and brings our focus down into our bodies to navigate our day with more ease. It's gentle enough even for babies, but its power is felt in each intentional sip.

◇ Lemon balm is one of the most brightening and soothing plant allies I have ever worked with. It eases fatigue and depressed energy caused by stress, and it smells and tastes amazing.

Nighttime Grounding Infusion Recipe

A relaxing and soothing herbal beverage to sip 30 minutes before bed.

◇ In your jar, pot, or French press, combine 1 tablespoon skullcap, 1 small teaspoon of lavender, and 1 tablespoon of passionflower.

◇ Top with recently boiled water and steep for 5-20 minutes. As above, if you used a mason jar, strain the herbs out before enjoying this infusion. Sip slowly and mindfully before bed, using this space for any evening meditation, ritual, reflection, or intention setting for your journey into dreamland.

◇ Skullcap is so nourishing to the nervous system, especially in times of stress and chaos. When I am moving through a tough time or painful transformation, skullcap is with me every step of the way to calm my emotional and mental bodies. She is wonderful to sip during the day or before bed to ease the mind, relieve tension, and soothe nervous or anxious energy.

◇ Lavender is one of the most accessible plants you'll find that also has numerous benefits. It is calming, cleansing, renewing, and uplifting to the spirit in a gentle way. She supports us in clearing the mind so we can witness the truth of our intuitive wisdom, and she also relaxes the body to ease stress and tension.

◇ Passionflower is wonderful for relieving tension and nervousness. I often get restless energy in my body before bed, especially if I spent too much time on my computer or phone throughout the day, and passionflower soothes it beautifully. She is also a plant that brings us home to the wisdom within our hearts.

These herbs are all pregnancy safe in moderation. If you are on any sort of medications, please consult with your doctor before consuming them. Nervines and some medications and alcohol often don't mix well.

TENDING TO

THE
EARTH

Chapter Four

The Elements

R itual connects us to nature and the seasons of change we witness within and without. Nature reminds us that life is moving through all in its natural rolling rhythms. It is through our ritual practices that we may understand the deep connection between ourselves and the elemental world around us. Medicine is abundant all around us within this beautiful, bountiful Earth we occupy—in the gentle streams of water filtering across grounding rocks that mirrors the blood that runs through our veins, in the wind that beckons change with each breath, and in the fires without and within that tend to our spiritual truths. Medicine is in the soil that assists our growth and the rains that tend to it and wash us clean like the tears that stream down our face. This medicine is the only tool we

need to live a life of healing, balance, and love. The Earth is our home. She is our body, that which lovingly holds us in this life.

All over the world our ancestors worked with the elements, respecting the medicine they so generously provide, worshiping the sun as God, the moon as Goddess, plants as spirit guides, animals as sacred teachers, flowers as expressions of self, and flowing waters as spiritual healers. They had profound connections with the natural world, communing with the land, moving in flow with the waters, and honoring all its cycles and rhythms as reflections of our own inner cycles. They understood that all we need is right here on Earth.

The elemental world invites us into relationship so that we may support each other in our sacred tending in order to live lives in connection to all that is sacred. When we take the time to connect with and tune into the Earth's medicine, we can remember this deeply encoded wisdom and connection. When we listen to and honor this relationship, a path of understanding will unfold, guiding us home to the heart's truth. We must develop a sincere commitment to the oceans, rivers, flowers, animals, trees, rocks, and mountains—each elemental spirit that guides and teaches us the true pathway forward to listen, to become soft, and to receive. The natural world holds us, responds to our needs and desires, strengthens us, grounds us, and supports our blossoming. Nature communicates just as we do. Birds sing their prayers to the wind, mycelia create networks of ancient wisdom beneath forest floors, and the relationship between the flowers and the bees connects all life together in a beautiful web of creation.

The elemental energies are our most trusting allies in ritual work and they will always be a part of our tending. They beautifully and powerfully assist us in cultivating presence, balance, and they support our healing always. It is through the elements that we find our sacred center—softened like water, fueled with fire, grounded on the Earth, our ear to the wind.

RITUAL TO CONNECT TO THE ELEMENTS

Grab a journal, get outside, and go to your favorite spot in nature. You don't have to go far—you can do this ritual in your backyard or local park. Set the intention to connect to the elements and receive whatever healing your spirit needs today. As you walk around or sit in this sacred nature space, take in the available oxygen with each inhale, feel the atmosphere, breeze, or the sun's warmth, absorb the healing ions of the Earth beneath you, and feel into the safe and grounded energy the elements provide.

In your journal, describe what you see, feel, hear, and witness intuitively–birdsong, flowing water, leaves in the wind, light filtering through trees, a sense of peace or play. If you can, go barefoot, with your feet anchored on the ground, or with your hands mindfully touching the elements (a tree, the ground, a flower, a stream or another natural form of water). With your hands or feet in or on an element, feel into the heart-beat of the natural world. Feel the waves of endings and beginnings that are guided by the momentum of time, all a part of the rhythm of the divine current. Attune your breath to these sacred rhythms. To attune ourselves to the elemental messages carried in subtle vibrations around us, we must be present and listen. Witness the sense of calm and centered presence that arises from this connection. Notice what subtle energetic shift you feel. Do you suddenly feel calm, supported, grounded, uplifted, inspired, wise, motivated, or more aware? Go deeper with that feeling. Where do you feel it in your body? You can ask for a message from the elements if you feel called. What sudden insights, wisdom, inspiration, or feeling floats into your being? This connected feeling is your truth, your birthright. Attuning to these vibrations can take time and practice, because it's not something we are used to doing in our daily lives. But being attuned to the subtleties of the natural world aligns us with all the magic and medicine it has to offer.

When you are finished, thank the elements for their presence, grace, medicine, and love. If you experienced a strong connection or discovery while doing this ritual, you may desire to bring a little piece of nature back with you to place on your altar—a flower, a fallen leaf, rock, a bit of soil or pinch of sand, a cup of river water, or anything else that speaks to you. Just remember, when taking anything from the elements, always give something back in return. With gratitude and love, restore balance with a song, hug, another elemental offering, nature mandala (more on this in chapter nine), some water, a strand of your hair, or anything else you have that feels sacred. If you don't yet feel comfortable in this exchange, read chapter ten for more about reciprocity.

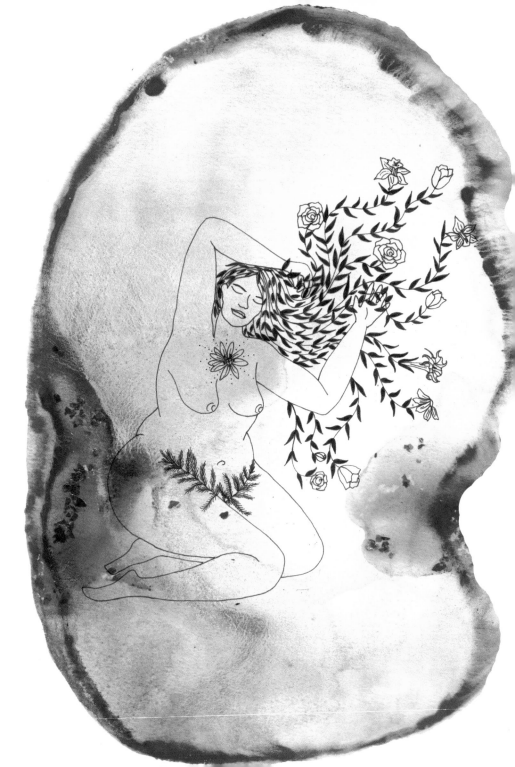

Chapter Five

Earth

Earth is the element that governs our physical reality. It's the most tangible, as well as the foundation that holds us in place and grounds us into being. The Earth is also a mirror for our body and physical health. We tend to the Earth when we need to anchor, to nourish our physical selves, and to move our energy from thinking into being. The Earth is also the element of death and rebirth, the darkness in which all grows, like the plants that wither and blossom again and again, from seed to winter's decay. The Earth teaches us purpose. It is our compass pointing north, guiding us toward the stability our soul is here to cultivate.

EARTH RITUAL

Our fear and separation from the natural world and our loss of this intimacy keep us from connecting to the wisdom of the Earth in our DNA. But all we need to do is free ourselves to the Sacred and remember. We have forgotten that the remedy for any ailment can be found within the Earth. We have forgotten that a flower will tell us exactly what we need if we ask. We are naturally designed to work with the Earth in this way. Along your sacred tending ritual path, your connection with the Earth will deepen, because it must. To begin remembering this medicine way, start by going out in nature and noticing what plants grow wildly around you. Wherever I go I am met with rosemary and roses—two of my closest Earth allies. These are the medicines that support my personal healing. We will find guidance in the medicine that shows up for us the most! When you notice a plant over and over, begin to connect consciously with it—sit with it, get to know it, and learn about its medicine and uses, ask if you can harvest a few stems or leaves of the plant, ask it what medicine it has for you specifically, place some at your altar, and when you feel ready, you can continue this work by making medicine with the plant. Here are some of my favorite ways to work with plant allies:

◇ **Infusions.** For plant-body nourishment. Dry out a few tablespoons of the leaves or flowers of the plant and steep with hot water for at least 40 minutes, or overnight, and drink slowly with intention.

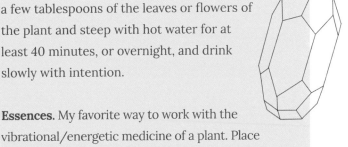

◇ **Essences.** My favorite way to work with the vibrational/energetic medicine of a plant. Place the blossoms or leaves into a clear jar or bowl of spring water sitting in direct sunlight for 2-8 hours. You can also do this under the light of the full moon, or both the sun and the moon. Strain out the plant and lovingly give it back to the Earth. Sip the liquid throughout the day, pour in a bath or over your body, put in a spray bottle and use as a face toner or aura mist. If you wish to preserve the essence and work with it daily you can combine 8 parts of the essence liquid with 2 parts alcohol (vodka or brandy that's at least 40 proof), place it in a dropper bottle and use it as a vibrational remedy by placing 3-5 drops on your tongue or in water a few times a day with intention and paying attention to the vibrational shifts that occur.

◇ **Herbal smoke bundles.** Gather the plants you connect most with and stack them together in a bundle, wrap with a natural cotton string or yarn, and burn with intention around your body and home as an energy shifter.

◇ **Fresh plants.** Placing fresh plants in water on your altar, laying them on your body while meditating, or brushing your body with the plant are all beautiful ways to bring the plant's healing essence and energy into your ritual practice. If the plant is edible, consider incorporating it into your daily meals for a boost of medicine.

Direction of the North: Guiding Toward Purpose

Some us come to this Earth remembering our purpose, but most have forgotten. This purpose might be to learn how to be a loving sister or father, to create a home to support others, to inspire the world in transformative ways, to lead, to make art, to express yourself with confidence, to heal ancestral karma, to clean up our Earth, to change the world with your gifts, to express love as much as possible, or to simply have fun and enjoy all that the Universe brings to you. It's important to understand that your purpose and your career are not necessarily the same. Although that may be the case for some, purpose is often much deeper than how we make our living in this life.

In our current age we are faced with so much that pushes us to forget our purpose. The media, our culture, and even our families condition us with judgment, fear, comparison, and doubt. But at its core, our disconnect from purpose is a disconnect from the natural world and the nature that we are. All we have to do to align with our purposeful path is simply remember and reconnect to the physical. Purpose is found by tending to the well of truth within your heart. Our souls chose now—this timeline of rapid awakening—so that we can radically change our collective consciousness and planet. Every single person is here to contribute to the healing evolution of our Earth and its species.

RITUAL FOR PURPOSE

Take a moment to think about all the animals of this Earth. Each species has a specially designed purpose that makes up the whole of the ecosystem of life on our planet. Animals have so much medicine to offer us and can teach us the instinctual and intuitive ways of life—the natural way of being. You won't see an animal trying to force its becoming or searching around trying to find meaning for their life. It simply moves and cycles and becomes and fulfills its purpose, because it is present in the now and adapts to life as it flows through it, their instinctual nature guiding the way. Working with animals in Spirit or simply observing and listening to them can guide us along our path and allow us to be more in tune with our own natural animal rhythms, as we are animals

too, flowing from the same source, just mani-
festing as different species.

From a comfortable position and quiet
space, connect to your breath and soften your
being. In your mind's eye, bring forward an image
of an animal that has been speaking to you lately, or
maybe always has. If nothing comes to you, take a
few more deep breaths and ask your subconscious to
show one. Don't overthink, just notice the first animal
that comes to mind. Take a few moments to observe
the animal and feel into its essence. What lesson or
energy comes to mind when you see this animal?
For example, when a deer comes to me, I think of a
gentle patience and calm grace to move forward in
life. When I see a snail, I am reminded to be slow and
mindful. And the bee—a favorite animal ally of mine—
reminds me of my interconnectedness and purpose
to support the hive with heart-centered action and
resilience. Everything we witness from the natural
world is a reflection of ourselves and a reminder to
align with purpose.

Take some time to notice what your animal looks
like. Is it male or female? Is it young or old? What
color is it? How does it appear to be feeling? These
details will reflect this essence within you. Communicate with your animal spirit and ask it to guide you
toward greater purpose in your life, showing you

the gentle way to flow throughout your path. Don't try to control or doubt whatever is happening, just allow your animal spirit to guide you and be in open observation. Take notice of any whisperings, messages, feelings, or sensations that arise. If nothing comes forward for you, just try again at another time, trusting you received everything you need in this moment by simply attuning your awareness to the medicine of animals at this time. When you are finished you can simply thank the animal spirit and journal out any discoveries.

Chapter Six

Air

Air is the element of communication and change. It teaches us to listen and connect to Spirit and its divine messages. You can connect to this element through your own sacred air—your breath—or through the breeze that whispers wisdom, or the howling wind that signals change and carries us into what is new. Air connects us to our inner voice of divine reason that leads us in a sweet dance with the winds of change.

RITUAL TO CONNECT TO YOUR BREATH

Your breath is truly your greatest healer. Like the wind, it has the powerful ability to move whatever is stagnant. Spiritual traditions all over the world speak about the breath as the gateway to unconscious healing—our path toward enlightenment. But how often do you pause to breathe—I mean, really breathe? Not the autopilot shallow breaths of everyday life (aka the survival breath), but truly allowing your breath to draw in large amounts of oxygen and healing flow. Breath is an essential part of any ritual or healing work. We not only need our breath to survive; we need our breath to heal, clear out old energy, return to our center, and remind us that we are here—alive and breathing. You can practice this exercise as a little pre-ritual or a ritual on its own.

Begin by taking slow, deep breaths, with 8 counts in and 8 counts out. Follow your breath as it flows in through your nose and down your body, your own life force energy coating your throat, heart, stomach, limbs, and toes. Allow your breath to soothe and relax your entire being. After 5-10 minutes or so of this slow and intentional breathing, open your mouth and exhale with a sound. Exhale all the worry, overstimulation, anxiety, and fear of the unknown. Exhale the future projecting, the hurt of the past, and anything keeping you from focusing on your breath in this moment. When we begin drawing in a lot of oxygen and focusing on our breath work, we can feel a little light-headed, tingly, or notice pains surfacing in the body. This is simply your breath working hard to go where it is needed, moving stuck energy, healing trauma stored in the body, and creating more space for love and consciousness to grow. When working with intentional breath, we can also visualize our breath going to where it is needed in the body. Not feeling grounded? Send your breath to your feet. Headache? Send it to your head. Trust your breath and allow it to connect your body and mind and offer you beautiful healing and support.

As the element of change, air's essence and wisdom teaches us flexibility. Allowance of change is necessary for growth. We must change our minds, change our beliefs, our ideas, relationships, even career paths and locations. Change is simply aligning with the natural rhythms of being, moving with the wind of our experience and courageously adapting to all that comes in with the night's breeze. Changing our minds to align with our hearts can certainly bring up discomfort. Society loves consistency and control, wanting us all to stay the same to support their structures and beliefs. But change is evolution. It's awakening more fully to passion and purpose. It's letting go of all control. The most beautiful thing about change and the wind is that they completely sweep us off our feet and carry us to new terrain.

Direction of the East:
Our Inner Compass

Wind is the element of listening. Not just to Spirit and its messages, but listening to our own inner compass and intuitive wisdom. Silence is a medicine that teaches us to listen. Silence reveals us to ourselves, allowing us to witness our truth. The ritual of silence can be very uncomfortable at first. We are conditioned to fear the unknown, to fear the truth, and even fear our own thoughts and emotions. Silence can open space for you to hear your shadows, your fears and insecurities, your roaring ego, your needs and desires, or anything you have not been listening to or holding space for. If you remain silent and listen, you will begin to hear the truth and find healing and power from that truth. Desires can have space to emerge and clarity can be found in these silent moments. We have to move past all the noise to hear what is true.

When you are feeling disconnected from your inner compass, give yourself the gift of silence. You may choose to start your morning with an hour of silence, go a whole day with silence, or get in bed twenty minutes early and just be silent—true silence means no phones, no books, no words coming in or out at all. Just inner listening. Just being. Whatever you choose, stay in your silence for as long as it feels right. Listen to the whispers of your heart. Witness all that is wanting to be said from within. Witness your fears, your pain, your desires, your inner wisdom guiding you. Just observe and don't analyze or try to process everything that emerges. Rest in this silence, holding space for grace and the way Spirit wants to move through you.

Chapter Seven

Fire

F ire holds the spiritual power of transformation. It holds our courage and offers us protection, purification, and profound spiritual healing. Fire is our passionate fuel that guides creativity. Fire can also carry sexual energy, anger, frustration, and the force that drives our ambitions. The element of fire can be used in your rituals when you need to transmute, purify, direct energy, activate, channel courage, or connect to your creative desires and passions.

Our inner fire is our sacred fuel—our spiritual light that drives us into action, expressing our truth in passionate surrender. Fire and dancing have been intertwined elements of human experience on this Earth for eons. Dancing around fire has been an integral ritual in human nature since the discovery of fire, practiced with intention all over the world. Movement tends to our inner fires and activates it in a sacred surrender. Dance and its flowing rhythms and emotional root have always been used as a powerful tool, activator, and expression of spiritual fire. Dance is the ultimate creative expression to connect us to the sensual pleasure of being in the human form—a practice that reminds us of the spiritual fire that is within. This is a powerful, simple practice that can be incorporated into your daily life as you learn to tap into the fire within. You may choose to call upon this ritual in times of transformation, to clear out stuck energy, ease stress, relieve anxiety, ignite inspiration, or fuel desire, passion, and creativity.

DANCE RITUAL

◇ Make a playlist of your favorite songs, get into your body, and move. I love slow and steady drumming, a powerful and inspirational voice, and lyrics that steer the body to remember that it is a potent tool for emotional expression, all woven with upbeat, hip-shaking tracks and heavy tempo beats throughout.

◇ Move mindfully and slowly for as long as it feels good, sensing into your body, noticing the sounds, feelings, smells, sensations, and messages. Allow each movement to be a prayer. Try lyrically stretching for

a few songs. And then, shake your body, throw yourself across the floor, take up space, wave your arms around fast and then slow and fast again. Stretch out your spine, get on the ground, bring all your energy, power, and light to your movements. Truly dance like no one is watching except for the Universe and all its spiritual guidance. Notice what movements feel good and any sensations as you move and activate your inner fire. Notice where your pain lives in your body, as well as your fear and your desire.

◇ From this spiritual rhythm, imagine a fire softly burning in your belly, unraveling a cauldron of passion and strengthening your connection to your spiritual power.

◇ When you are tired, lay down and just breathe. Further feel into the sensations of your body and all its power. Place your hands on your belly and breathe into that space.

◇ Thank yourself, the music, and the Sacred for tending to your inner fires today.

Direction of the South: Transformation

Transformation propels us into new ways of being. It requires courage, faith, and connection to our spiritual fire. The sun is an element of fire that reminds of us the courage and passion burning within. In many spiritual traditions, the Sun is considered to be an expression of divine masculine power. When we work with the sun as medicine with intentionality and reverence, we can absorb all its sacred healing, fiery fuel, motivation, and passion to walk through the fires of life.

SUN RITUALS

◇ **Sunrise sun gazing.** Wake up for sunrise and gently look to the horizon as the sun's light begins to slowly rise and offer its healing light to our day. Before the sun is fully awake in the sky, it is safe to lightly and softly gaze into its light at the horizon. This is a powerful ritual that fuels us with a lot of energy and vitality. It's more energizing than coffee!

◇ **Sunbathing.** I am sure you have sunbathed before, but have you tried it naked and with a healing intention? Our bodies don't get the vitamin D and sun's kisses as much as we should. We are actually taught to fear the sun in our modern culture and lather our skin with chemicals to prevent our skin from absorbing the sun's naturally healing energy. When the sun can reach the parts of our bodies that are usually closed off and hidden from its light, we can offer those spaces and their energy more vitality, strength, and healing. Do this just 10-20 mins a day in early daylight before the sun is at its strongest midday, flipping half-way on each side of your body. As you soak up the sun's energy, set your intentions, say your prayers, or meditate to create space. If you get too hot, stop and go inside. You may have to vary your times depending on where you live and how hot it is. Your body will tell you when it's had enough. Sunbathing our crystal or plant allies by laying them in the sunlight for a few hours is another beautiful way to bring the sun's energy into our ritual practices.

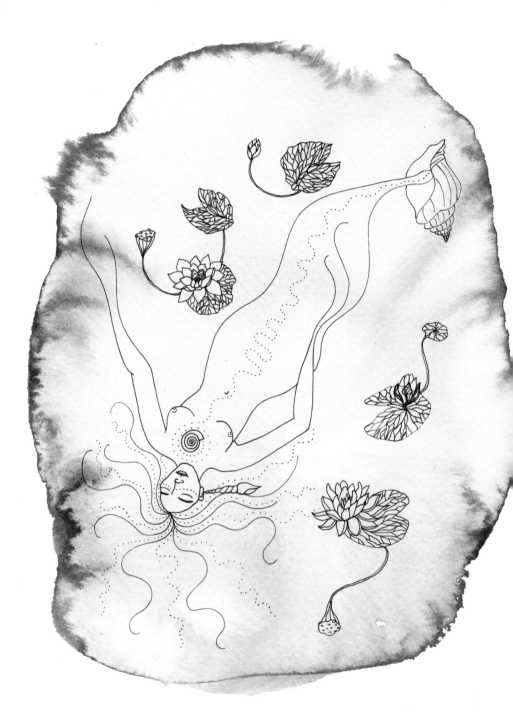

Chapter Eight

Water

Water is the element of receptivity, healing, inner wisdom, and cleansing. This energy governs our heart and emotional energy. She is cooling, calming, and wild. We use the element of water to soothe pain, move emotions, connect to our intuition and our well of soul memory, and open to receive the energy of love's embrace.

Water is sacred and thoroughly connected to the holy. It carries the waters of our soul and the rivers of our heart. In mythology, wells are often gateways between worlds, and in Celtic traditions they are holy healers. Water is our most healing emotional ally, washing away our worries, fears, and repressed emotions. Water opens the heart of belonging and love spills out in flowing healing rhythms.

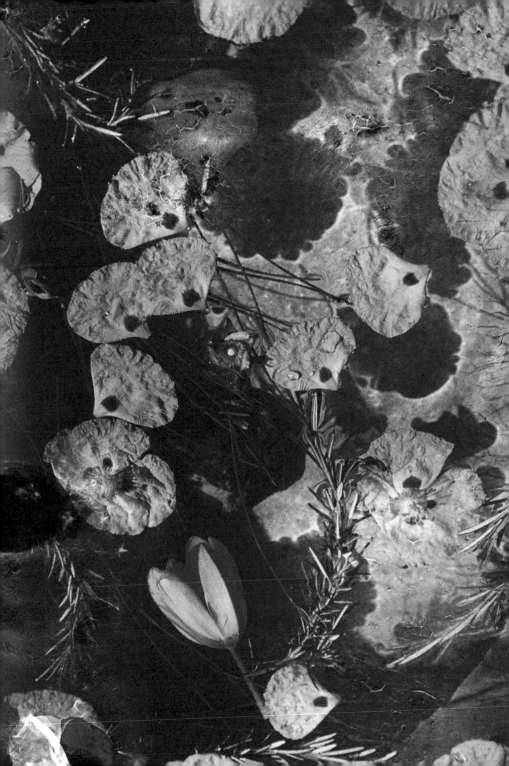

WATER RITUAL

When we are disconnected from our inner waters, deeper feelings, love, cut off from receiving, or just in need of healing support, we don't need to look any further than connecting to the element of water. Water brings our emotions to the surface and offers us a safe container to allow them to flow and express. Emotional healing is profoundly personal, so for this ritual, allow yourself to be permeable in the hands of water's loving embrace. Allow yourself to really connect with your intuition and be guided in a state of healing flow.

Connect to water by drawing yourself a bath or going to your local watering hole (ocean, river, creek, stream, and so on). Allow yourself to be guided toward wherever your heart is feeling called. If you are unable to travel to a body of natural water or do not have a bathtub, a simple bowl or bucket of water, hose, or any form of natural water will do. At your water element, hover your hands over its surface. Ask this water to open your heart and assist you in healing and cleansing your being. You can set the intention for any specific emotional healing you are seeking.

Open your heart and give your water an offering. Maybe it's your tears, a song from your heart that you sing into the water, some rose petals, or a crystal—whatever you feel intuitively guided to do here. Song and sound are highly activating for water. Your heart will feel itself echoed in the water, so allow the heart to be your only guide. Once your offering is given, cleanse yourself with these healing waters—dunk yourself in, pour the water over your head, sink your hands into it, drink the water, or do whatever is accessible and makes sense for the water element you have connected with. The more surface of your body that gets watered, the better, but even just connecting to the water intentionally will have a healing effect. Let go of control and allow the waters to cleanse your being and assist your heart in opening.

Once watered, place your hands on your heart and take a few gentle breaths. Remind yourself, "I am healing, I am love, I am loved." Allow yourself to hold space for whatever emotions arise. They may come up right away or things may begin to move in a few days. Allow the waters to teach you to surrender any resistance. Just trust your inner waters and take gentle care. Thank your water and continue with your day in whatever way feels right.

The Way of the West: Connection to Intuitive Waters

Water is a direct link to our intuition, our inner sea of wisdom. It is deep, unknown, both dark and light, wildly reflective, ever flowing and ever knowing, containing thousands and thousands of years of magic. Did you know that only 5% of the ocean has been explored? That is indicative of how much of our inner waters we have explored as a collective. Our inner intuitive waters are our power, our guidance, our true knowing and wisdom stirring within. Our intuition speaks in a unique language only we know and only we can uncover through our sacred tending. Like exploring the ocean, discovery of our intuitive gifts takes time, courage, and trust as we surrender to the dark depths. Intuition and fear naturally duel within, that's why it can be a challenge to hear and trust our intuitive wisdom. Fear keeps hidden what we do not know and are afraid to explore, just like the depths of the sea. But when we are connected to our inner waters of knowing, we can move in our natural flowing rhythm like the water that teaches us, with integrated wisdom and love. This is one of my favorite rituals to use the element of water to connect to intuition:

MOON WATER

⬦ Fill up a mason jar or clear glass with clean spring water.

⬦ Drop in one smooth, cleaned, tumbled moon-stone crystal to assist you in connecting to your intuitive waters. You can also use any clean tumbled crystal that you feel connects you to your intuition. Labradorite, amethyst, and iolite are all good options.

◇ With your hands on the glass, set the intention that this water will assist you in connecting to your intuitive wisdom. Remember to anchor into your heart with trust and belief in your ritual. You can say a prayer out loud or in your head, or write down your intention with any symbols you connect with and place the paper under your container.

◇ Cover the container with a cotton or silk cloth or lid.

◇ Place your crystal in the water under the light of the moon for 2-8 hours. The moon guides the waters on our Earth as well as our inner waters, so connecting to her is a beautiful way to connect to this sacred intuitive power.

◇ When the time is right, sit with your moon water, remove its cover, and drink slowly, mindfully, and intentionally. I like to do this ritual in the evenings or first thing in the morning. Do this in silence and with pure presence and observation, no judgments or analyzing. Try to focus your mind on stillness and just take

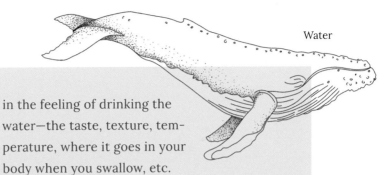

in the feeling of drinking the water—the taste, texture, temperature, where it goes in your body when you swallow, etc.

◇ Thank the moon, the waters, and your crystal for guiding and supporting you.

◇ Journal anything that comes up for you during this process and be open to further intuitive insights that begin to surface.

Chapter Nine

Reciprocity

Tending to the natural world is essential. We can no longer ignore or expect the Earth to just be there giving us all that we need, shutting out her cries. Her resources are limited. She is our mother, and she is burning, melting, and roaring in a call for help for us to tend to her needs. Animals are becoming extinct and others are abused and mistreated for profit, as are our trees—our sacred lungs here on Earth. We are meant to connect to the natural world as if it were a friend, a sister or brother, mother or father. We are all a part of the same Earth family. The trees need the air we exhale, yet we forget that we rely on them to breathe, as well. We forget, so easily, just how important this relationship is for our mere existence. Our connection is such a simple act, but we've completely lost our intimacy with the natural world as a collective and it's begging for us to return to this harmonious kinship.

The Earth is our mirror—the truest reflection for our collective. Its self-destruction and decay shows us the separation we've created with it, with ourselves, with all that is Sacred, and with each other. When she burns, it mirrors the repressed anger we are holding from not meeting the needs of our Spirit, for not listening to truth. Her polluted oceans reflect the pollution of our inner waters—our disrespect and dishonoring of the emotions and intuitive wisdom of the feminine. The remedy is actually quite simple: conscious communication, love, and connection can help restore this balance. Once we each form a relationship with our elemental allies, our awareness will shift to honoring and protecting, and change the way we relate to the natural world as a whole, just like a connection with any growing relationship. Our future depends on how we tend to the Earth today.

When working with the natural world in our healing, we also must cultivate a relationship with the land that supports us where we live. We thrive when we are connected to and work with the land that holds us. Simple ways to do this include:

◇ Spend time with the land. Listen to it. Get to know its natural features, its seasonal blossoms and cycles.

◇ Research and recognize its indigenous origins. Who lovingly tended to the land before you? How can you honor these people? Are they still active in your community? How can you support them?

◇ Join a local land conservation group.

◇ Try to source fresh herbs in your community or in the wild, instead of bought in plastic imported to your grocery store. Look for community gardens, farmers markets, CSAs, or even plant them yourself! For dried herbs and plants not native to your bioregion, check out your local apothecary to support small Earth-conscious businesses. Always ask where they get their herbs and if they are sustainably harvested or organic.

◇ Plant walks are also a great resource for learning how to spot medicine in the wild so you can forage yourself, and they can also teach you more about what grows near you. Find a local herbalist who you resonate with and support them.

Ways to Further Reciprocate

◇ Talk to the trees like a friend. Ask them for guidance and support and listen with care and respect.

◇ Plant trees and flowers. Reforest and replant. Revive our dying plant species.

◇ Stop utilizing single use plastic, especially if you have a company that sells products. Our oceans are drowning in plastic and our sea creatures are suffering. We are disrupting balance because of our addiction to consumerism. Plastic does not disappear and most of it

doesn't get recycled. You can nowadays find a plastic-free alternative for almost anything you could ever need with a little bit of conscious attention. Do your research and be mindful of your plastic consumption. Choose consciousness over convenience, the larger vision over a quick fix.

◇ With everything you take from the Earth or that is made of the Earth, say a simple thank you before using or consuming it.

◇ Say intentional prayers and blessings for the Earth and her healing.

◇ Withdraw your support from companies and groups that are not in support of the Earth's health and sacredness— companies that use unsustainably harvested resources or unnecessary plastic, those that engage in unethical farming, and fast fashion.

◇ Share with friends and family how to be more eco-conscious. Does your mom recycle? Is your brother still using plastic straws? Does your best friend need an iced coffee served in a plastic cup every day or can they bring their own cup to the coffee shop? Gently offer suggestions to support the Earth whenever you see fit.

◇ Support companies that focus on Earth connection and protection. We vote with our dollars and money is energy. Give your energy to those supporting the Earth.

◇ Always harvest from the Earth (even picking a dandelion from the sidewalk cracks) with respect and care, and always leave an offering to the Earth in gratitude for what you take. This can be in the form of a song, a prayer spoken out loud, native seeds, water, etc. Sit with plants before harvesting them, and always ask the plant for permission, only taking if you intuitively feel it's okay (for example, do you feel an expansive light or joy in your heart, or can you only feel uncertainty?). Take only what is needed, allowing the plant to regenerate.

Throughout this book I hope you will cultivate your own powerful connection to the Earth and her medicine. The ritual below can assist you in cultivating this sacred exchange between yourself and the natural world that surrounds you.

EARTH ALTAR RITUAL

Traditionally, a mandala is a graphic depiction of the Universe, usually in the form of a circle—a complex symbol with no end and no beginning. It represents the connection between ourselves, the Earth, the cosmos, and Spirit—the infinite cycle of this sacred life. Creating a mandala as an offering to the Earth is a beautiful and creative way to honor this connection and offer your love to the Earth and all she gives every day.

◇ Go out in nature with a cloth bag or a basket.

◇ Begin to explore and just observe the natural world around you. Notice the colors, textures, and shapes around you.

◇ Begin to collect little treasures of the natural world around you—a twig, leaves, flower petals, pebbles and stones, wood chips and bark, even fruit. Follow your intuition and choose whatever you are guided to with love and intention.

◇ When you feel like you have gathered up enough materials, find a sacred space that you feel drawn to to create your mandala. Choose a spot you can visit often, and return there to replenish the offerings you give to this altar. Maybe it is at the base of a tree, in a garden, at the beach, or by a stream.

◇ Start from the center and build outward, placing item after item in a circular geometric pattern. There are no rules. Let your creativity guide you and express your love through the Earth elements. As you place each offering, make sure you set intentions of healing, love, connection, peace, or whatever else comes to mind. Singing can carry your intention and love as a healing prayer. When you sing to the Earth,

she hears you, and it is a beautiful
way to offer your love while you
create. When you are finished, place
your hands at your heart and notice
how you feel.

◇   Take a moment to connect to the Earth. How
does she feel? Can you sense her gratitude for
your presence? Ask the Earth for a message for
how you can support her. Just be open to receiving anything that comes through.

◇   Give thanks to the Earth and allow your mandala
to offer beauty and love to all beings that come
across it. Return to this space to replenish your
offerings as much as possible, repeating this
ritual. Slow, intentional moments of connecting
and tending to the Earth bring us back to our
inherent oneness.

Chapter Ten

Our Mission, Our Healing

We are all divine souls living a human experience. We all come here with a soul contract—a sacred mission or divine purpose to heal, to evolve, to become, and to offer our wisdom to the world in exchange. Our individual lessons and life paths are unique according to what specific areas our souls need to grow in, but we all come here to remember who we truly are, why we are here, and to remember that life is sacred. We also come to learn devotion, how to love, and to free fear into the light. Tending to the Sacred is our truest mission on this Earth and it all begins with tending to the Sacred within. Our inner work is a part of the collective mission to create harmony in our world. We change the world from the inside out. When we dedicate ourselves to our healing, we find the strength within our own beating hearts and the sacred songs humming through the rivers of our bodies. Ritual is a simple, powerful, practical tool to connect to our sacred holy essence and remember the Higher Self—the truest essence of self—without the fear, control, and judgment that keep us further from sacred love. Ritual helps us to reclaim all parts of the self once forgotten, returning us whole.

When we are disconnected from the Higher Self, it shows up in our bodies. Physical health is the foundation of spiritual health. Our bodies require us to be in intimate communion with their inner intelligence. But if we don't learn this as children, how do we teach ourselves? As I mentioned before, we can see the root of this collective wounding directly mirrored in our Earth's health, too. Her basic needs for survival are not being met for her vitality. Let's face it, we are collectively unhealthy and neglected/neglectful, and most humans aren't intuitively connected to our Earth or our bodies like our ancestors once were—in the way we naturally are designed to be. Full health and vitality, courageously following desires and passions outside of limiting systems, feeling comfortable in our bodies and trusting in Spirit are all rare ways of showing up these days. This is why tending to the self—inner listening and taking care of our individual needs and healing—radically changes our lives. When we learn to meet our needs fully, listen to our bodies (and not through diets, trends, gurus, or looking to others for answers), and give our bodies exactly what they need, we evolve. Our bodies move into their natural rhythms of homeostasis with full vitality, and we gain the energy to align with purpose, passion, desire, peace, and love.

For self-tending ritual work, you don't need a healer or anyone to "fix" you to obtain your own spiritual and physical harmony. You are all you need. Your body, your breath, your heart, your awareness—you. Learning to listen to your unique needs is at the root of self-tending. If we grow up with our basic needs neglected, we tend to neglect them as we age. Sadly, it often takes illness, disease, or an accident or injury to take our unique body's needs (and the emotions that animate them) seriously and tend to ourselves. As you move further into this book and your own inner healing, it's important to check in with yourself, your body, and your needs often to see if your patterns, routines, diets, relationships, ways of being, and even (and most importantly) healing rituals are still serving the needs of your Higher Self as you evolve on your path, as you and your needs are always evolving. Tending to ourselves ripples out and reflects every person, place, and opportunity that comes into our energy in exchange. Collective healing is a domino effect. Heal ourselves and then heal the world. This is the most sacred work of all.

The most important thing to cultivate as you dive into self-tending is presence. Presence is the state of simply being—in the now, attuned to what you see, smell, hear, and witness through your body in your heart. The gift of presence is better than all the gold in the world. It awakens our heart to the sounds of grace and connects us to the natural flow of life. If we place our attention on emotions of the past or on fear of the future, we are giving our energy away, which means there is no vital energy available for the present moment, and the present moment is essential for our ritual work and a life of grounded ease. When we anchor in the present moment, we call our energy back to ourselves and return home to our physical body and our beating hearts. The lack of presence is what creates anxiety and an overstimulated nervous system, which often leads to lethargy, a taxed adrenal system, health issues, and depression. In order to heal and move into balance, we must learn to be present with our emotions, our fears, our aches and pains, our desires, our needs, and every ritual act we perform. If you struggle with settling into being present before a ritual, try connecting to all your senses. Our senses ground us in the now when we see, feel, touch, smell, and taste life and all its many facets. Practice taking a few breaths and noticing your present environment through your senses, allowing them to guide you back to the now. You can also connect to any of the practices listed in chapter three.

Chapter Eleven

Self-Healing

You don't need any training in order to be your own healer. Healing is a way of life with love as our north star guiding us home. Healing energy is universal and available to all, with the source channel being our beating hearts. Healing touch is a technique that has been used for thousands and thousands of years to provide solace to those in need. Our hands have meridians of energy constantly flowing with love from the humming of our sacred hearts to the touch of our fingertips. Healing touch brings awareness to the energy of our bodies and can help to release trauma, stuck energy, and emotional blocks, and to cultivate awareness and presence.

If you are in need of healing support, know that you are enough to provide it. Simply sit or lie down comfortably, center yourself by connecting to your breath, bringing your awareness to your heart and feeling the energy of love, and place your hands on any area of your body where you feel you need healing. Just allow your intuition to guide your hands. Connect to your breath and anchor into love as you focus on sending love to that part of your body for as long as you want. You may feel sensations in your body, have sudden insights or emotions come to the surface, or maybe you simply drift off into a deep rest or meditative state. Allow all released energies to flow out and be recycled back to the Earth. When you are finished, express gratitude for your love light for being your healer.

This practice allows us to bring our attention and awareness to ourselves and to what needs healing, and that can then guide us in being more in tune with our bodies, energy, emotions, and empower us to hold sacred space for healing energy to flow.

Tending to Our Shadows

When we bring ritual into our lives and become closer to all that is sacred and to all the love that is available to us, we must be willing to look into the mirror and face all that has been keeping the Sacred hidden in the dark behind curtains of fear, pain, control, and distrust. Fear and trauma live in the shadows of our self-tending. Our shadow self is the darkness—the denied and repressed. It carries those emotions we reject, the spaces within where we feel unworthy, the basket of fear untended to, and all those things we were told were wrong or bad about ourselves. It holds the pain from where we were not loved by the people whose love we desired most in our lives. Most of all, it shows us all the places we are not loving ourselves. It houses our traumas behind closed doors and carries ancestral karma hidden in dark closets.

The most important thing to recognize in this tending is that our shadows aren't bad. We only fear and reject them because they have been rejected by others. It is normal to have shadow and wounding. It is normal to feel shame and fear—it is a part of being a human! This human experience is both shadow and light. There is no joy and peace without pain, no expansion without contraction, not life without death. Sadly, shadow is rejected in most spaces, but we are moving toward facing our wounding and healing and reclaiming shadow for the Sacred in our collective healing. Death leads to rebirth, and we can only access love and light as much as we have grieved and held space for the messy, painful moments of our spiritual healing. When we face the shadow self, which is always trailing close behind and showing up in the way we interact with others, we can learn to integrate those rejected and unloved aspects, accept our shadows, and heal into a state of wholeness. When we block out our shadows from witnessing the love in our hearts, we keep ourselves disconnected from our truth and cannot show up in life authentically as our whole self, worthy of love despite fears. When our shadow is controlling and blocking out our inner light, we may overreact, blame others, carry too much imbalanced fire,

not take accountability for our faults, have a hard time seeing any side but our own, lack compassion for others, or become overly defensive and resistant when triggered. When we hold onto shame for having shadow, this also prevents our ability to dive into the shadows and offer them healing.

We are all whole at our core. No one is broken, no soul is void of love. Our souls *are* love! But we must tend to our inner wounds in order to bring ourselves into this state of wholeness. We must intimately know and witness our shadows to know how to tend to ourselves. Rituals assist us in taking time to witness how we truly feel instead of letting old shadow patterns tell us how we feel. This work is what you will tend to again and again and again on your spiritual path.

To begin to witness your shadow, notice how you speak and interact with yourself and with others. Ask yourself, "Is this my wounding speaking?" often. Notice what triggers you most in others. For example, my shadow holds a lot of controlling judgment because of the criticism I received in my early life. I tend to project this shadow onto others when I am not in a whole, integrated state, and project it even more on myself with chronic perfectionism and control whenever I am in a space of fear. Because of what I endured in my upbringing, I was imprinted with a conditioned belief that I am not worthy just the way I am, that I always need to change or fix something about me to receive love and be worthy of what I desire (which, of course, was always love). My conscious mind knows this is not true, but my unconscious shadow self needs to be loved and reminded whenever she emerges from her depths. When I notice my shadow coming out, even if it's just in my mind with internal dialog triggered by something, I know I need to tend to her and

bring her to the light, because this untruth disconnects me from showing up as my authentic self.

The most powerful moments of your spiritual evolution happen in the abyss—in the wild unknown, the dark shadows of your experience. These moments of healing are tended to on the floor in messy emotional surrender, visiting the darkest spaces of our psyche. When doing shadow work, we can't be afraid to get our hands dirty and experience the fullness of our inner darkness. Profound healing requires you to face your fear and to feel your wounds.

When doing shadow work for the first time, I highly recommend creating a support system that includes your favorite self-care rituals (baths, self-massage, naps, other practices included in this book), a physical support system (friends, family members, therapists), and allies of comfort (plant, animal, and Spirit) to call upon if things feel heavy or confusing. Before going into the shadow ritual, take some time to journal out the questions below. Journaling out specific memories and experiences may help in this process. You may wish to do this at your altar, with a candle lit, incense, or soothing sounds to help you drop into this sacred space.

BRINGING SHADOW TO THE LIGHT

At night before bed, sit or lie down in the calm darkness. You may wish to wear an eye mask for this, but it is important that it is dark. Find softness and ease in this dark space. Set the intention to heal and integrate your shadow, finding light and softness in the dark. Close your

SHADOW JOURNALING

1. Take inventory of all the places in which you resist loving yourself.

2. What are all the lies you have been told or have told yourself?

3. What traits or ways of being do you find most triggering in others?

4. What were you not loved or accepted for as a child that you wish you were?

5. What are you insecure about that you wish didn't matter?

6. Where do you wish to be more confident?

eyes and begin to connect to your breath, breathing in and out slowly and mindfully. In your mind's eye, visualize a dark cave before you. As you enter the cave, go deeper and deeper within, and allow your shadow self to greet you. This is the version of yourself that is wounded, driven by ego, repressed, unloved by you and others, or just begging to be noticed and integrated. Sit down in the cave with your shadow self. Notice any details—your shadow's fears and thoughts and feelings, or maybe what they are wearing and how they appear. Hold space for whatever comes up, accepting them all as your own.

As you sit with your shadow, call in and visualize black-eyed Susan flowers creating a circle around you and your shadow. Allow the energy of this flower medicine to bring beauty and light to the shadow within. Ask the flower to help integrate your shadow into aspects of light, seeing the gift and strength your shadow self provides. Visualize your shadow self merging with you, absorbing their full essence of divinity, reclaiming the pain, the wounding, and all the fears and ego. Give your shadow the love and full acceptance it so desperately desires. Feel into this essence of wholeness, the shadow and the light of you—a perfect balance of Sacred love. When you are ready, exit the cave.

Thank the Earth and your shadow for assisting you with your healing. Open your eyes and journal out everything you experienced and felt during this meditation.

Using this ritual as a frequent practice can help bring awareness and integrate aspects of yourself you are rejecting and stuffing down—all that prevents you from healing and moving closer to truth and wholeness. All of you deserves acceptance. We cannot be accepted by others until we learn to accept our whole self, accepting all the lessons and medicine and messy moments that come with the territory of this life of blossoming. These shadow spaces are where the richest soils live, where fertile seeds of abundant growth may be planted.

Chapter Twelve

Self-Love

The foundation of healing is coming home to yourself. Self-love is the true path to liberation, radiance, and inner peace. It not only requires us to face the parts of us we may feel are ugly or not worthy of love and acceptance, but also to radically love them. Self-love requires us to honor our wounding, pain, and also our pleasures, desires, life path, and needs. Without self-love we will cater to others over our own passions and choose fear over love, shame over reclamation, judgment over honor, self-doubt over empowerment, and struggle over abundance. Love is our birthright, and without directing this energy toward ourselves, we can never truly be in our power. We can never truly be lit up by life and its limitless possibilities for us.

Our souls chose these bodies, this time, this experience for us to learn. Our stories are crafted by our choices as we grow. Choice is our greatest power of all. Choosing self-doubt and judgment over self-love is the most dishonoring thing we can do in our lives, yet we all do it all the time because we are constantly told we are not good enough. Women and minorities especially are repressed, judged, shamed, abused, dishonored, told to be quiet, to stop taking up space, to not do things differently, and to not speak truth. We are all more powerful than you could believe, and despite what we were given, we are the creators of our realities. We attract into our lives everything we need in order to step into our fullest power and heal, and self-love is that path. When we direct love toward ourselves—and stand fully in our light of love and honor ourselves for the beings of love we are—we find grace.

Our lack of self-love leads to a lack of self-worth. When tending to our shadows, ourselves, our inner love and healing, we will find all the areas within where we feel unworthy of what we seek, whether that be love, security, or a new job. Self-worth is the magnet that draws everything in life to us. A balanced person with healthy self-worth will attract dreams, love, and all that they feel worthy of in life. There are no limits when you believe you are worth it. A healthy self-worth transforms fear into faith and self-trust. A person with low self-worth will attract people, places, things, and opportunities that reflect that low worth. This could manifest as being underpaid at their job, relationships that don't value them, scarcity, and struggles of all sorts. Finding our inherent worthiness is one of the most powerful lessons of healing we will ever learn—to know in our bones that we are here, full of love, and worthy to be, following our inner compass guiding us toward the dreams burning in our hearts, all the desires we once feared were too big or too much. On your path you will reach down and get to know your true value and honor it.

Forgiveness

The only way we can truly heal is when we look at our wounds directly, bringing them right up to our face and accepting and forgiving what caused the wound in the first place. Forgiveness is truly one of the most powerful allies in healing. Not just forgiving those who have caused us wounds, but forgiving ourselves. When we look at the past with forgiveness and acceptance we can anchor into our grace in the present and peel off the layers of wounding to reveal a more authentic, whole, bright version of ourselves that is grounded in truth.

SELF-FORGIVENESS RITUAL

◇ Get a bowl or bucket of water (whatever temperature feels comfortable for you), some fresh basil, and fresh rosemary. Both basil and rosemary are beautiful cleansing herbs that assist in clearing out wounding and stuck energy while fortifying our energy field.

◇ With your vessel of water, sit outside on the Earth. You may choose to be naked or in a bathing suit, to sit on a towel or just have one next to you.

◇ Lovingly and intentionally hold your herbs in your hands, connecting to their energy, their smell, and their medicine. Inhale their scent and allow it to infuse in your body.

◇ Place a few basil leaves and rosemary sprigs into the water, stirring them around with your hand as you speak your intentions for self-forgiveness into the bowl. As I mentioned before, water is highly activated by sound, so speaking your intentions out loud or singing to your water will be a beautiful addition to this ritual.

◇ Take a few deep breaths, and when you are ready, slowly pour the water over your head and allow it to wash you clean.

Forgive yourself for feeling that you are responsible for others.

Forgive yourself for your past self. They are a reflection of who you were, but not who you have become.

Forgive yourself for being in relationships not in alignment with you.

> *Forgive yourself for trying to be someone that you are not.*
>
> *Forgive yourself for carrying shame and guilt projected onto you by others.*
>
> *Forgive yourself for giving away your power.*
>
> *Forgive yourself for being human.*

If there is someone you need to forgive other than yourself, try writing a letter to them. It may be a parent, a friend from the past, or a coworker. Remember to anchor in a space of love as you write, leaving out any blame, but saying what you need to in order to feel in your power and authentically you. You don't have to send the letter unless you feel called, but the simple act of intentionally offering love and forgiveness to this person while anchoring into the four pillars of ritual can allow any resentment or victimization energy to dissolve, opening the heart to greater love and trust.

To forgive, we must truly accept things for what they are or were. The energy of acceptance is like a healing balm we can offer ourselves and others. It creates neutrality and peace. Not only do we need to accept others for their own journeys, but we must accept ourselves for where we are and how we feel every day. Acceptance allows us to find presence, peace, and to grow with more ease, trust, and love.

Chapter Thirteen

Self-Protection

When we begin to heal and connect to presence and the Sacred, everything in our life changes. By tending within, the outer landscape of our reality transforms. We may notice that we are highly sensitive to things we once didn't think twice about. We may find that we can no longer hang out with the same people, consume the same things, talk about certain subjects, or be in the same environments. This experience can be jarring at first, but it is perfectly safe to be sensitive in this world. We just need the right tools to navigate our paths with our sensitivities.

When I began connecting to ritual and deepening my spirituality, becoming aware of my sacred truth, I suddenly developed strange food allergies and experienced other health issues (my

body's favorite way of teaching me something is out of alignment). Eventually I found myself having an anxiety attack at a job that was not in alignment with my truth and feeling sick to my stomach when I hung out with people who didn't have my best interests at heart. This is the power of awareness. It is not that we suddenly develop an intolerance to a thing; it's more that we become aware and present with our space, body, and energy, as well as how things affect them. Now, in our world, we can't avoid every little thing that feels unsafe or stressful. We may still have to take crowded and loud public transportation to work, communicate with family members who are difficult for us, or simply see or hear the news. But what we can control is our spiritual strength, boundaries, and rituals for self-protection, and these allow us to navigate difficult spaces with ease, fortified in our love's healing and protective essence.

Boundaries are our greatest tool for self-protection. Boundaries are formed when we say *no* (and mean it) to anything that doesn't immediately feel like a *yes* or helps us feel safe and good. Having boundaries means that we no longer settle for dynamics that drain our energy or do not meet our needs. In order to fully connect with our inner authority and wisdom—and move into alignment on our spiritual paths—we must declare boundaries with our time, energy, space, body, encounters with others and relationships, personal needs, and consumption. Some examples include:

◇ No TV after 9pm, because it makes it hard for me to fall asleep.

◇ I will no longer talk to this person if they cannot treat me with the respect I deserve.

◇ I will no longer scroll through social media accounts that feel judgmental.

Boundaries show the Universe that you care about yourself and your healing. This is self-protection.

Intention is also a powerful ally in self-protection work. Simply connecting to your heart and setting the intention to self-protect will strengthen your auric boundary. When we believe we are safe and supported by Spirit—as well as connected to all that is Sacred and the love in our hearts—we find protection and energetic fortification. Ritual assists in our self-protection, acting as a healing barrier between us and anything that is not in alignment with us. The ritual below is one of my favorites for when I need some boundary support.

RITUAL FOR BOUNDARIES

Find a comfortable and relaxing space where you will not be disturbed. Clear your space with the smoke of your favorite plant ally. Sit or lie down, close your eyes, and connect to your breath—allowing your breath to soften your being into a gentle and relaxed state. Set an intention of self-protection, and specifically include anywhere you are struggling to form firm boundaries in your life.

In your mind's eye call upon the energy of yarrow
by visualizing the plant. Yarrow is a healing balm of
protection—the salve of strength—and known for
millennia for its powerful medicine. In Greek legend,
Achilles used yarrow to heal his soldiers, and he
bathed in yarrow before battle to make him nearly
invincible (the plant's name, Achillea millefolium,
means "Achilles' thousand-leaved plant"). Imagine the
many leaves of the yarrow creating a wall around your
entire body, acting as a powerful protective barrier.
Feel into their energy of protection and support.

Out loud or in your head, ask the spirit of the plant
to create a firm energetic boundary around your aura,
keeping out all the energies not aligned with your being
(anything you picked up from the day that is not yours to
carry) and strengthening your connection to your inner
authority and truth. Feel into the strength and fortification as it arises. You may notice you sit up taller, spine
still and strong, or you might become aware of some other shifts in your body and energy. When you are finished,
thank yarrow for its medicine and carry this energy with
you through your days. Repeat any time you feel you
need support in honoring your boundaries and energy.

Energy clearing is another form of self-protection. We can call on
various allies to assist us in clearing our energy (some of which I
spoke about in the Space section of chapter one). When we clear

our energy, we remove any fog keeping us from being anchored in our love. For that reason alone, it is important to connect to allies from the heart that inspire love and connection to the self. When clearing energy, always remember your breath and intention. Here's a list of daily energy clearing practices I use:

Personal Practices

◇ **Visualization.** I use visualization in multiple ways in my ritual practice, and I highly recommend it for anyone. One way I like to use this energy clearing tool is to visualize a golden light glowing in my heart and then see that light extending out to my aura to protect and secure my energy. Sometimes I will also visualize it expanding up and out around my room or house to clear and protect my space as well as myself.

◇ **Prayer.** Prayer fortifies us through the energy of the words we speak. Here's an intentional poem of the heart I sometimes use in order to connect me back to my sacred home within: "I am protected by the light of the Divine, the energies of love that surround me and are within me, always. I am protected from all energies that are too dense for my light body and anchor into my truth and sacred love." Song is another form of prayer I use in my daily practices.

◇ **Breath.** I have already spoken about the power of the breath and its ability to create space, but it can also fortify and protect our energy field. When I feel uncomfortable or anxious, I always return to my breath—four counts in, slow through my nose, and four counts slowly out through my mouth, repeated four times. The number four carries a grounding and fortifying frequency—just think of a square and its solid four sides creating a container of protection that blocks out anything else from entering.

◇ **Practice saying no.** No is your strongest boundary creator. I think people often have this idea that spiritual, love-centered people are simply nice and only devoted to service to others. While that may be true to some extent, spirituality and love are also fierce, firm, and not always easy to digest. I have had to turn down countless people and opportunities over the years because they didn't align with me. Had I said yes, it would have been a disservice to both parties. I have broken hearts, quit jobs suddenly, blocked numbers, cut people from my life, canceled clients, and declared strong boundaries in my work time and time again. These acts were to support my needs and the greater good of all. If I am not supporting my needs, I can't show up the way I need to in the world. When any opportunity comes in that doesn't inspire you, say no. When someone asks you to do something that makes you feel uneasy, say no. When a friend wants to gossip about someone you care about, say no. Say no to outdated beliefs and habits. Say no to draining environments. Say no to people who ask a lot of you without respect for your needs. Say no to people who don't honor your worth and undervalue your time and energy. Anything that doesn't feel like a yes in your heart—anything that doesn't light you up—say no. Verbally setting your boundaries in life is a powerful tool that you will use time and time again throughout your journey. The more you say no when it feels like a no, the more space you create for the things that draw a yes from your being.

Self-protection is something we can call upon whenever we feel afraid, suffer from a lack of security, experience doubt or confusion in honoring our boundaries, or feel disconnected from our inner authority, Spirit's support, and the Sacred within.

Chapter Fourteen

Self-Expression

Self-expression brings us pure heart expansive freedom! Sharing ourselves in whatever ways we need—creatively, emotionally, verbally—is one reason why we are here. Your vulnerability is your strength and power. It can be terrifying to share ourselves in an authentic, raw way, but Spirit supports us in doing so, always. Our stories heal and connect us. Our truths allow us to thrive. Our voices light up our paths and the paths of others. Our art heals the world. The world is waiting for your true authentic self-expression. So much is available when we just say yes to the passion burning within, begging for release.

One of my favorite rituals to open up the energy of the throat—the seat of our authentic self-expression—is to intentionally spend time humming, singing, or chanting. You can intentionally feel into the sound vibration from your heart, belly, vocal cords, and lungs, dissolving anything that cages your voice, allowing yourself to move into a fuller expression of you.

The Inner Child

At the root our authentic self-expression is our inner child. Our child self is in alignment with our most authentic expression. As children, we play, sing, and dance without fear. We express ourselves emotionally, verbally, creatively, physically, and uniquely in the way that is authentically in alignment with our spirits. We explore, ask questions without fear, imagine, create worlds of magic, and love without limits. Unfortunately, as we age we are silenced—shut down by the harsh realities of modern life with all its limitations, shame, and ideas of who we are all supposed to be. To align with our most authentic expression, we must learn to tend to our inner child, let them out to play, to explore, to see the world through a magically inspired lens, and to speak their needs and desires to us. Tending to the inner child is a lot like learning to be our own mothers and fathers, giving ourselves the love and freedom we need to grow.

INNER CHILD RITUAL

Set the intention to connect to your inner child and create a space for them to come out and play.

Maybe put on some music they loved, or wear something that reminds you of them. Invoke your inner child by finding joy in simplicity, silliness, and joyful expression. You may choose to sing, play outside, or do something your child self loved to do. Let your imagination run wild crafting stories and dreams, or maybe spend time playing with any children in your life. Children are the best medicine for connecting to and healing our inner child. Let go of responsibility and limitations, and just allow yourself to relax into the joy of playing for as long as it feels right. You deserve to play and express. Allow this playful expression to act as a healing balm for any wounding your inner child carries, especially any wounds related to them not feeling able to just be themselves.

Creative Expression

You are a walking embodiment of creation—always changing and evolving, just like nature. Your unique creative juices run through your veins just waiting for you to notice their pulse of inspiration. Creativity is a pure and sacred gift of this holy existence. Everyone is an artist. Being an artist does not mean making art for a living as a career—that is just a label society has created to fit people into certain categories and further create separation.

Creativity is one of the most basic human instincts after eating, sleeping, and being safe. Nothing would exist without the energy of creation. We are here to remember that we are both the art and the artists of this life, crafting our desires lovingly as we tend to the sacred wells of creative inspiration within. Healing is creative and creativity is healing. Through our creative exploration, we can find what our unique medicine is, as well as how we may bring it to the world. And awakening to our creative power is how we envision and craft a new world.

When we allow ourselves the freedom to create without the limits, judgment, and perfectionism that get in the way of what wants to purely spill out from within our beating hearts, art is truly the best form of therapy. Creativity allows us to integrate the energies of desire and love and bring something new into form from those energies, guiding us to more fully understand and express our inner world outwardly. More than talent, creativity simply seeks authentic intention from the heart. It doesn't matter if we are technically good at our chosen expression by some external definition—if it's created from the heart, our work will be felt by others and will offer healing to those open to receiving it. We can bring this intentional creative energy into everything we do—cooking, dressing ourselves, decorating our homes, or expressing ourselves in whatever medium feels best in any moment. Bringing creativity into the mundane amplifies our lives and invites in more beauty and pleasure.

As an artist, I am always creating. When I am not creating in some way, I tend to get frustrated or feel repressed. For this reason, I try to make everything in my life art, for that is what life truly is—even the mundane. For example, I love to create my own cleaning products with my rosemary and baking soda, oils, and lemons. When I do this, cleaning becomes a sensual experience with the plants, free from any of the chemicals I am sensitive to. Or, if I have a lot of computer work to do, I spend some time creating magical, beautiful teas and

treats for myself before sitting down to work, in addition to dressing beautifully, creatively, and intentionally so that I feel grounded and inspired. Cooking is another way I infuse creative magic in my life. Most every day I go to my garden to feel inspired by the plants. I will harvest while singing a gratitude song, and creatively alchemize a beautiful, medicinal meal to nourish my body.

Ritual is a form of creativity in its own right. When we create art in a ritualistic way, it only becomes more powerful and healing to those who witness it. This is one of the reasons I felt drawn to tattoo art as a medium of my expression. As you now know, everything carries a vibration. When you create an intentional, medicinal, high-vibration image with the energy of love, the receiver of that image will then match the vibration of the image and the intention behind it. Tattoo art is powerful for this because the image stays in our skin and works through us constantly, changing our vibration and altering our life through its healing, but all art can have this power when the four principles of ritual are involved in the creation process.

Take the image on the left. My intention when creating this drawing was to inspire creativity and uplift the heart. When making it, I said a mantra that supported this intention and connected to the universal energy of creation and love. I believed in the power of this image and further activated it with my hands and my heart, visualizing the energy it would activate in others.

Tune into the image and meditate on it. You can visualize the image imprinting on your heart, or imagine yourself breathing in its energy. You can also trace this

image and place it on your altar for the week, sitting
with it and connecting to its intention anytime you
come to your altar. Take your time to feel into any
messages or energy it awakens in you. Remember,
energy work is subtle and requires patience, presence,
trust, and a receptive heart. I encourage you to explore
this ritual on your own, creating your own intentional,
healing art and seeing what it invokes from within. Play
with colors, sacred symbols, plant and animal medicine,
words, shapes, and anything else you feel a vibratory
connection to for your healing.

Calling Forth Our Desires

Ritual helps us learn that we no longer have to wait to create the
lives we desire or the changes we need to live a life of passion and
freedom. We are creating our lives in every moment. Every action,
belief, and thought is rippled in the unseen and has an effect that
can be felt in our physical reality. Manifestation is connecting to
our creative essence and calling in that which we desire with those
same authentic energies of the heart. If you are not happy or comfortable in the life you are in, you can weave yourself a new web—
one of free expression, aligned opportunity, love, and whatever
else you authentically desire from the deepest wells of your heart.

All that we desire in this life is a direct message from Spirit to go
toward it. You can think of passion and desire as the map toward

discovering your purpose. Whatever you love—whatever excites you or you are truly passionate about—there is a reason for it. Denying our desires is to deny ourselves pleasure and passion. Denying desire leads to settling for less, unfulfillment, lethargy, and often suffering. If it is a yes in the heart or the gut (basically anywhere in the body but the thinking mind), it is a yes from the Universe.

Disconnection from desire is not uncommon. When we navigate life based on our conditionings or fears, we cannot feel our desires burning within. An essential part of our spiritual journeys is awakening to our unique desires and pleasure, and being courageous enough to follow their energy each day.

MANIFESTATION RITUAL

Manifestation occurs when we combine desire, action, and receptivity—a beautiful combination of our feminine and masculine energies. This is needed for creation. If you paint a picture, you need the vision and creative inspiration, but you also have to pick up the paintbrush and get to work. The picture doesn't paint itself. If we just dream and envision with no physical application, then the inspiration stays in the ether and isn't grounded into form. On the other hand, if we are just doing—that is, putting all our energy into action and forcing things without the feminine juiciness of desire and without the ability to receive what we want—then we will create friction. This creates struggle, burnout, and for many female-bodied people, unbalanced hormones and health issues, as females are designed to be naturally more receptive. The energy simply will not be aligned for the creation to come in. We have to be able to truly feel into our feminine energies in order to co-create with the Universe, to let go a little, and to open to increased trust and love, but not be so passive that we aren't doing any of the work required to receive what we want. Here's a ritual to help that:

◇ Make a cup of hibiscus tea, light a candle, and take some time to journal out a list of all the things that light you up—any desires and activities that excite you, make you feel passionate about life, and stir inspiration within, and especially those things you have always loved doing since you were a child. Your list can include anything. It could be as simple as "smelling roses" or "cooking dinner for my family." As you are journaling, make sure you are being as authentic as possible, removing any ego or judgment around what you are writing down. Your list holds the key to your divine purpose. It is your guide to lead you toward all the things your soul is asking you to create—the map to all your dreams. You may have one thing on your list or twenty-five, it doesn't matter as long as it is true to you. Feel into the energy of each desire on your list. How does it make you feel? Imagine your body as a chalice. As you read off each item on your list, your chalice gets filled more and more with a rainbow of light. Allow the desire, pleasure, and excitement to move through you. Before going to the next step, over the next few days I recommend that you create more space to do those things on your list and that you take small action steps toward them. If smelling roses is something that sparks passion and pleasure in you, maybe you weave rose water or rose scented oil or candles into your daily rituals. The idea here is just to connect you with the things that light you up and to help you feel into the experience of being connected to desire. It is essential to be committed to our desires in order to receive them.

◇ Next, make a list of your dreams—the big picture vision for your life, everything you truly want to call forth. Maybe it's a love partnership, that dream job, a new home, to grow your family, community, a trip across the world to a land that is calling you, or an exciting creative opportunity. You may be as detailed or nonspecific as you feel is right for you, but focus on the feeling, allow your desires to be the way-showers. If you don't know exactly what it is that you want, take some time to go within, connect to your breath and intention, and ask Spirit to show you. Don't doubt what arises. Whatever it is you are dreaming of in life, it is 100% attainable for you on your path. Only your limiting subconscious beliefs prevent it from actualizing. Tend to the Sacred and open your heart and mind to your soul's possibilities so that you may receive these gifts.

◇ Under each dream, write down any fears or limitations you feel are preventing you from aligning with each one. Write down as many things you can think of that are stopping you from being open to receiving your desires—fears of not having enough money to quit your job and try to find a new one, a lack of self-trust to believe you can pursue art as a career, low self-worth that prevents you from going after what you want, fears that what you want doesn't want you, a concern that others will judge you for being different, and so on. Identifying what is stopping us tells us where we need to heal, so allow yourself to go deep within for this step. You may find that meditation or a ritual for grounding or space clearing can assist here.

◇ In healing these limitations, the first step is awareness—identifying what is holding us back from what we truly desire, then feeling through the emotion that arises from that space. Take time to read through your limitations and fears and identify how they make you feel. This could trigger some pain, guilt, fear, anger, or shame. Feel through whatever arises, as this is an essential part of making space for your desires to come through. You may choose to connect to water or do the Ritual to Open to Love from chapter one. If no emotion surfaces right away, give it some time and maybe journal through what comes up for you some more, allowing yourself to explore more thoroughly with tender care. Take time for as much self-tending ritual work as you feel you need as you uncover any wounds and begin to feel yourself come into wholeness, recognizing your limitations as a part of your shadow self, but understanding that they no longer control you and that you are now choosing your heart's truth over your conditionings, fears, and outdated stories.

◇ Now let's focus on the energetics of receiving. Light a candle and set the intention to call in your dreams and desires. Sitting up with your spine straight in a comfortable seated position, close your eyes and focus on your breathing. Imagine that all of the limitations you just journaled out are now dissolving from your body and moving down into the Earth beneath you. Continue this for a few moments, letting go more and more with each breath, until you feel a sense of clarity. Then, bring your attention to your heart and send your breath there, allowing the heart to soften and open with each breath, breathing in and out the energy of love. Now, imagine the thing you want most is approaching your auric field, visualizing it about six feet in front of you. Hold this image for a few moments with presence and focus. When you are ready, say the following out loud: "I open my heart to receive all my dreams and desires wanting to come into my life. I am committed to releasing all that stands in the way from receiving what I want and I trust in Spirit's guidance to lead me along the way." If you feel any resistance when verbalizing those statements, repeat them a few times until you really believe it. When you are finished, blow out your candle and say thank you to Spirit, who is always listening.

◇   This process takes patience but can lead you to reclaim your creative power and fully receive all that you want in life. Repeat the above whenever you feel blocked from receiving something you are calling into your life or feel confused about what you really want. Trust your process and trust your desires. Big manifestations take time. Both my dream forest home out of the city and this book took two years of deep healing, committing daily to my dreams, and tending to the Sacred for them to actualize, but the things that helped them become my reality the most were trust and commitment. Little things will manifest more quickly, and everything will vary from person to person depending on their unique shadows and wounding. Trust your journey and trust yourself.

◇ Remember to be open to witnessing all the joy you have already created in your life and open your heart to all that you will create. Focusing on lack and scarcity will keep the things we desire further away from us. Gratitude and joy for this present moment allow us to be open to receptivity.

Be Seen

The fear of being seen because we don't feel good enough is one of the more common reasons we are unable to go after what we want, express ourselves fully, and show up in the way our soul is leading us to. The fear of being seen relates to the fear of our shadow

selves and inability to see and love our whole selves. It's where we are unable to witness all the sacred beauty within. When we hide a part of us that we consider to be unloveable and refuse to look at our true selves, we end up shrinking to fit in smaller roles in our lives. To be comfortable being seen we must learn to be comfortable seeing ourselves fully—all our beauty and all our flaws.

Self-portraiture has been my most healing ally in tending to this fear. I grab my camera most often when I am moving through healing shifts. I go out into the beauty of nature and shoot from a present and embodied space of being, capturing the changes unfolding within and without myself on film. I allow my body to flow and bear witness to its intuitive movements and remind it that I love it. I am quickly reminded that my body and my heart have carried me through many selves—my arms hold others, the soles of my feet connect me to the heartbeat of the Earth, my womb has moved through death and birth, my lips kiss and scream and speak my truth, and my green eyes, like my grandmother's, are made to see the beauty and sacred truth in all aspects of life. Seeing beauty in myself has shaped the way I perceive the whole world around me. This self-portraiture practice is a ritual I have done since I was a teenager and probably one I will never abandon, because of the powerful healing it provides.

To try this ritual yourself, first set the intention to witness your power, beauty, strength, wisdom—whatever you are unable to see within yourself. Grab a camera (or paints, pens, or whatever creative medium you feel called to) and truly see yourself and capture yourself. If you are not using a camera, get a mirror to lovingly gaze at yourself or dance in front of it. Notice your softness, your hard lines, the hue of you, any freckles that lace your skin, the "flaws" you have been judged for and the beauty that lives beneath them, the emotion behind your eyes and the love in their subtle movements. You are a work of art. Allow your creation to remind you of that. Tell yourself "I love you" as you create, and mean it. You are enough.

Chapter Fifteen

Self-Care

Checking In

Before going any further, let's check in and take inventory of the heart and body. In your journal, answer the following:

◇ How is my heart feeling today? Is it tender, strong, stuck in an emotion, raw, or steady?

◇ How does my body feel today? Do I feel heavy or light? Slow or fast? Watery, bloated, disconnected, strong, grounded?

◇ How can I be more gentle with myself today? Do I need a break or need to rest? Would it be most helpful to take time to listen, or integrate? Is it time to mother myself or allow more ease?

◇ What do I need to do to feel more grounded and centered today? Do I need to spend time outside? Where do I feel off-center?

◇ What nutrients does my body need today? Greens, iron, protein, fats, more water, any specific herbs or vitamins?

◇ How can I ignite joy and create more space for pleasure today?

◇ What is different about my experience today than previous days and months? Am I more present, more loving, more accepting, less anxious?

SELF-CARE RITUAL

The nervous system is designed for our protection. It is our body's communication center, our interface with the world—sending messages that allow us to think, feel, process the world around us, and move through it. This system is responsible for our fight or flight modes, but it also stimulates our body to function properly and gets it to relax and rest. If you spend most of your time stressed, reacting to stressors, and suffering from depletion, then a little extra nervous system support will go a long way. We cannot be fully grounded in the body and move through our awakenings until we heal this system. The good news is that if you treat your nervous system like the delicate, sensitive system it is, you can move throughout your life feeling centered, protected, grounded, and empowered—even in stressful situations or significant changes. If you are a highly sensitive person, tending to your nervous system is a necessary act of daily self-care.

One of my all-time favorite self-care rituals for tending to my nervous system is herbal body oiling. Anytime I feel tender or off-center, unable to see my worth, disconnected from my body, overwhelmed, taxed, or stressed, this is the ritual I turn to. Body oiling gifts us immediate relaxation and deep nervous system healing. Our nerves instantly absorb the fats in the oils through our skin, blessing us with a layer of protection and guiding us toward more body resilience. Bringing plant medicine and fats directly into the skin—our largest body organ—is a nourishing and grounding self-care practice. With all the stimulation of the modern world, body oiling can act as a filter between all that has happened in the past and all the future projecting into tomorrow, and bring us instead into the now—washing away the day and coming home to ourselves despite whatever has happened and whatever may come.

Herbal body oiling is a practice our ancestors used all over the world for centuries and centuries. Whatever we put into our skin goes through our lymphatic system and works to heal and cleanse our entire body. Whether you body oil for stress, for immune health, for dry skin, or for winding down at night, this practice can benefit anyone anywhere of all ages, no matter where they are in their journey. This ritual can be modified using the ingredients that you connect with and those most accessible and healing for you.

◇ Before beginning, decide which plants you want to use. You can choose a single plant, or you may like to choose three or four. Think about their medicine, their energy, and what intention they will bring to your oil. Always make sure they are herbs that are safe to ingest, as you will be taking them in through your skin. We never want to put anything on our skin that we wouldn't eat.

My favorite plants for body oiling are rose, lavender, kava kava, St. John's wort, rosemary, cedar, and jasmine. Though you can use fresh plants to make herbal oils, I prefer to use dried to prolong shelf life and prevent any mold from growing from moisture in the plants as the oil steeps. Fresh plants will require a slightly different process, so if you are gathering fresh plants from nature around you, allow them to dry out in the sun or hang dry upside down in your home for a few days until fully dried before using. You will want your dried herbs to be chopped or blended into small pieces, as well. A food processor or blender on low usually works for this. Be careful when blending hard roots, stems, and branches— petals, leaves, and other soft plant bits work best. Your local apothecary may also have dried herbs already available.

◇ Choose a carrier oil. I alternate between organic sesame (quite warming and great for cold environments, circulation, or winter months) and organic olive oil for its accessibility, preservation, high fat content, and ancient medicinal uses. Other effective oils include jojoba, avocado, coconut, and sunflower.

◇ Fill a glass mason jar about 3/4th of the way full with your finely chopped plant matter. Size does not matter—it just depends on how much you would like to make. I usually use a quart sized jar.

◇ Slowly and intentionally pour your oil over the plants, covering all plant matter, and filling your jar almost full, but not quite. Leave at least a finger or two at the top.

◇ Next, slowly stir your herb oil for at least 5 minutes, using this time as a little meditation and taking a few moments to set your loving intention of healing for your oil. You may wish to pray, sing, recite poetry, or play soothing music to your oil. Plants respond beautifully to music!

◇ Place the lid on your jar and come back to it a few times throughout the day and turn the oil upside down and right side up, over and over, like you are turning an hourglass. You can use this time to repeat mantras, prayers, or intentions. After plenty of mixing, fill the jar up all the way so that the oil now touches the lid when you place the lid on. You want to make sure there is no room for air.

◇ You will be steeping your oil for one moon cycle, so be sure to check the date and moon phase and mark your calendar for the next time the moon enters the phase it is now in. You may wish to start this practice on a new or full moon, but any day is fine. Full moons are my favorite days for medicine making. You may also wish to place your oil out under the moonlight some evenings to charge your oil with the moon's energy. Otherwise, label your oil with the plants and the date created, and store in a cool, dark place.

◇ Be sure to check your oil every few days as it steeps, and top it off with more oil if the level goes down. Air can cause mold to grow, especially if you use fresh plants. If you start to see any mold growing, skim it off with a spoon right away. In my experience, I have only seen this with fresh plants.

◇ At the end of your moon cycle steeping, it will be time to strain

your nourishing medicine. The next part is
a little messy, but have fun with it! Grab a
second jar that is the same size and place a
strainer or funnel over the mouth of the jar,
with a cheese cloth or woven natural fabric
such as linen or muslin over the top.

◇ Slowly and intentionally pour your steeped oil over
your empty jar, straining out the plant material
but allowing all the abundant medicine to filter
through. You can hand squeeze out the plants
at the end to make sure you get every last drop
of medicine available. When strained, make sure
there are no plant particles left in your strained oil.
Sometimes I repeat this process a couple of times
until the oil is clear, but I find every batch is different depending on the oil and plants used. You can
recycle your oily plants in a healing bath ritual for
your feet or entire body after your oil is strained.

◇ You can also add a tablespoon of vitamin E oil
to your strained oil to prolong its shelf life and
add extra nutrients.

◇ You can then transport your oil into smaller
dropper bottles as a gift to any loved ones who
may need this medicine.

◇ With your beautiful, healing plant oil, tend to yourself in ritual as needed. You can add a couple of tablespoons to a healing bath or light a candle and lovingly give yourself a massage before bed, paying close attention to any spots of tension and pain. You could also rub the oil on your feet and then cover with socks to ground you when you get home in the evening, or cover your body in the oil as you bathe under the sun. Connect to your intuition always. This oil is your medicine and your body will call for it whenever it needs its love and intention.

TENDING TO

THE SACRED

Chapter Sixteen

The Sacred

B eyond the controls of the mind, layers of existence unravel in soft waves of light, trickling out from beating hearts into warm hands, life spinning round and round in this magical, nonlinear, infinite existence of love and creation. This is the Sacred in motion. The Sacred is not one specific object, persona, holy figure, place, or something we need to collect or accomplish—it is a universal essence of being, a vibration and feeling we can invoke from within and witness in everything. This feeling of sacredness is love in its highest, purest form— without bounds, without any fear or resistance. This love—a holy feeling greater than the mind can comprehend—is the source of all things in this wild life. The Sacred is all that passes through

your body, your lungs, your mind, and your soul. The Sacred is in every tree, every person, every butterfly that whispers to the flowers, every spirit that burns in passion, every blade of grass that kisses blessings at your feet, and every star that shines down upon you lighting your path. Everything in existence is moved by the Sacred—the fuel of love that this sacred life is made of and for.

When we live paths dedicated to all that is Sacred—to the love in ourselves, each other, the Earth, and Spirit—we find a strength and balance, a knowing swirling deep inside. When we tend to the Sacred, the Sacred tends to us in loving exchange. The only thing that limits the sacred love and creation available for us to witness is our lack of awareness or fear of witnessing the infinite potential of the sacred, loving experience we are here to behold. It's often a fear of the unknown, of what we cannot perceive or understand with logic, that keeps a distance between our hearts and the Sacred. But ritual gives us the space to know the Sacred in our hearts—not our minds—and allows us to witness the Sacred all around. Ritual reminds us that nothing is separate from the Sacred. To come back to witnessing this multidimensional essence of being, we need only to connect to the four pillars of ritual: intention, space, love, and belief. With ritual we may learn to witness with our hearts the unseen threads that connect all things together in this beautiful web of life.

We are all vessels for sacred divine Spirit—stardust in bones, magic hearts and holy hands that thread our stories through this world. Accepting that sacred divinity is within us can take some time to integrate, for it is not a concept we are taught to know. Instead, we often learn through various religions that the holy is outside of us and that we must follow the rules in order to claim and know some of the love for ourselves, but this couldn't be further from the truth. There is nothing about this essence that is linear, one-way, or that we can reach with just our minds. The way to the Sacred is through gently tending, unknowing all the untruths, and awakening to your whole holiness—simply being you, loving fully, letting love in fully, and following whatever inspires your heart and lights up your path to live liberated and true.

Ritual assisted me in claiming the Sacred, recognizing it as not only something outside of myself in the stars, in the ancestors, in goddesses, and in spirit guides, but within myself. I realized how powerful it is to create space to connect to the Sacred, to feel the Divine pulse through my inner waters of love, and in turn to make space for more divinity, more love, and more prosperity to flow. When you can reclaim the Divine as a part of your own essence, you become one with all that is Sacred.

ILLUMINATING THE SACRED RITUAL

Gently close your eyes. Slow your breath to connect to the breath of the Universe—a steady and deep breath, in through the nose and out through the

mouth. Set the intention to illuminate the Sacred within. As you take in each breath, visualize and feel love and light pouring into your being. This can manifest as your favorite color, a divine archetype, plant or animal ally, a feeling, a sound, or a word. Allow your symbol of light to be whatever it needs to be and bring you into your sacred truth at this time. This symbol may change the closer you become to the Sacred—allow it. Allow it to merge your inner and outer worlds into oneness, into love. From this nonresistant state, open your palms face up, empty yourself with your breath, and ask for the Sacred to fill where it already abides. Sit with this energy for a few moments and move your hands over your heart. When you are finished, simply open your eyes and move throughout your day holding onto this holy essence, feeling into your sacred essence of being, and witnessing with clear eyes the Sacred illuminated all around you.

Chapter Seventeen

Connecting to Our Sacred Guidance

We are guided in each moment by our divine team of support. This team looks different from person to person, but may consist of animal guides, plant kingdom guides, star beings, ancestors, past selves, soulmates, angels, the souls of children you are yet to have, gods and goddesses, ascended masters, elemental spirits, "mythical" beings, planets, and so on. When we have a relationship with these guides, we can receive and feel this sacred guidance anytime we are in need. Guides will come and go as we evolve on our path, but no matter what, we always have support. When a guide shows up for us, we are to learn from their essence of being, their spirit. They become our teacher, our way-shower, our ally of support.

For example, when I was going through a painful contraction and expansion along my journey, I started to see the Hindu goddess Kali Ma in my mediations, and she even showed up in my day-to-day reality. Right at the same time, my first employee synchronistically came into my life bearing a Kali arm tattoo, because Kali was her teacher and favorite goddess. Kali is the wild feminine—the goddess of destruction, but a powerful symbol of both creation and devastation who symbolizes that we cannot have one without the other, and that these energies lead to our liberation. Kali Ma guided me as I experienced a big death and simultaneous birth in my life—a time when I stepped more fully into my creative power. As I was in the abyss—the dark womb of the mother inhabited by Kali—I called upon her energy for strength, power, and clarity when the challenges were heavy, and she showed me the way. By doing this, I attuned to her vibration and was able to feel her influence through me. I became the essence of Kali.

The faeries also visit me often in dreams and meditation when I need to dance, play, laugh, and create with my inner child. Ascended healers and medicine masters will come to me when it's time to learn a new skill, and they teach me through my meditation practice. I view whatever plants that show up around my home as allies and teachers, and I sit with them and often make plant medicine to strengthen our connection if I feel guided to. When I see an animal in mediation or while roaming the land I tend to, I know they are a guide, as well. I observe how the animal moves and lives and attune myself to their medicine by moving throughout my life in a similar way. As I wrote this book, my elemental guides and ancestors of the Earth and Cosmos spoke to me through my spirit communication channels. I consider this book to be written by me, in my voice, but also in the voices of all the guides and ancestors who have guided me. These are just some ways in which guides and allies can show up to teach us their ways of being, but the possibilities are truly infinite.

Spirit wants to talk to us and guide us on our paths—we only need to allow Spirit in. It is important to not doubt and dismiss what is unseen. We can't see air, but we know it's there keeping all alive, just vibrating at a higher speed than the density of solid physical objects. We must learn to raise our vibration to match Spirit's. Whatever we receive from Spirit is what we are meant to witness, and judgment will only stop this flow. The veil between worlds becomes thin during ritual, in sacred space, or in a meditative state, and that's when we can begin to witness the unseen and receive their messages.

Communication

Communication is the most important thing in all our relationships, whether with loved ones, coworkers, the Earth, or Spirit. Without communication, we cannot have intimacy, and intimacy is crucial on our sacred tending paths. Intimacy with our sacred guidance is what keeps us feeling supported.

The most common way Spirit communicates with us is through synchronicity. Synchronicity lives in the patterns and signs that show up in numbers, names, words, deja vu, symbols, strange occurrences, people, and dreams that have no logical explanation. These signs always show up in the way we each uniquely navigate the world, making their way into our awareness in ways we will notice. For example, that bee I mentioned at the start of this book was a beautiful synchronistic message from my guides. Had I not already felt connected to bees, I wouldn't have received the sign as strongly as I did. My guides would not have sent me a strange bird that I had no connection to, because it wouldn't move me as profoundly.

Because of my connection to the elemental world, I personally find these synchronicities and messages of guidance in the spider that crawls across my floor as I open my eyes from meditation, the snake that crosses my path on a hike, and in the rosemary, roses, and other flowers that follow me constantly in a way that always tells me I am supported. Synchronicities may appear for you as literal signs you see out in the world, subtle whispers or sudden insights, a message you overhear in passing or in conversation with a friend, in the animals and flowers that show up unexpectedly, and in whatever other ways speak to you.

We tend to this communication in our ritual practices. You can always intentionally ask for a sign to offer support in times of change and beyond by simply saying out loud or writing in your journal, "Guides, please send me a sign to [for example, show me I am making the right decision]," or whatever else resonates with your energy. Be open and aware in the following days and weeks to witness the messages that roll in with the wind. With this practice, you can form a more intimate relationship with Spirit and your divine team that guides you along your journey.

Having shrines for your guides is a good way to feed their spirits as they feed you. Love—one of the four pillars of ritual—is the bridge that connects us to being able to receive the guidance and support we seek. When you are in a long-distance romantic relationship, for example, it's common to create extra space to tend to that relationship to make up for the lack of physical one-on-one time you have together. Our spirit relationships are a little like this. You can think of a shrine as the phone line for sending your messages of love to strengthen your relationship. For example, I have a shrine to my late grandmother in my studio. Everyday, when I settle into the space for the day, I light a small candle under her framed photo and place fresh flowers or her favorite snacks there a few times a week. On this shrine I also have a bottle of her French perfume and a piece of her jewelry. When I want her to come in closer to me, I leave additional offerings such as a song, other favorite foods (rice crackers), prayer, play her favorite music (Prince), or just talk to her. This feeds her, and our communication line becomes clear. Instead of feeling like she is off on the other side of the world on a tiny island with bad reception, it feels like she is just in the next room calling out to me. You can do the same with any spirit guides of your own. I also make shrines for the bees, hummingbirds, ancient ancestors, goddesses, roses, elves, and fae, and I often change out the shrines when I feel a new guide who wants to work closer with me.

This is an important practice in your sacred tending, for feeding Spirit in this way feeds all that is sacred. It amplifies your intentions and calls in Spirit's support. I tend to make offerings daily, but I am sure to leave offerings to my guides and guardians before, during, or after any rituals to thank them for supporting me.

Sacred Symbolism

When finding meaning in all of the signs, sacred symbolism, and messages of guidance that fall into our paths, we must look within. No matter how many books or websites on symbolism we consult that decode all the colors, animals, and plants that show up for us, the truest meaning is found in our own intuitive guidance. Our intuitive language is like a dictionary of sacred knowing that lives within us, colored by our own experiences and energy. Connection to this language is what will support us most in receiving the messages that show up. Our intuitive languages are all unique, and this is why it isn't in alignment with our true knowing to seek the meaning of signs outside of us.

I'm often asked about the meaning behind the symbolism in my art, especially in my Soul Tattoo® work. What something personally means to me or a specific client won't necessarily be the same for others. This is the gift of having unique intuitive languages, medicines, and knowings encoded within our souls. For me, roses tell me to come home to my love and sensuality. They make me feel safe, whole, and grounded. When you see a rose, it could be a sign from a grandmother who loved roses, or a message to "wake up and smell the roses," or something else entirely different. Your guidance will come through in what you already know within, so there is no need to seek answers from without.

Our own journeys of self-tending will teach us to develop our intuitive language. As you enhance your receptivity and connection to your spirit guidance, you may wish to keep a journal as a dictionary of all you discover. I have done this with all the plants I have journeyed with, the animals that speak to me, and the sacred symbolism that I discover along my path of remembering. This is the resource that my Soul Tattoo® inspirations and illustrations come from. When I see a symbol in a client's aura, my intuitive language tells me exactly what it means and what medicine that client needs to integrate from the symbol. It is often an instant download that anchors into my inner knowing. Some symbols that come through can't be found in any book or internet search—they are too ancient, and some come from languages lost to history. I find these to be the most powerful and unique symbols, even if I don't always completely understand them right away.

Here are some examples from my personal intuitive dictionary. Remember that there is no right meaning for any sign, element, or symbol. They are always meant to speak to us individually. As you go down this list, think about what each one means to you uniquely.

◇ **Roses.** Unconditional self-love, truth, the sacred home within, connection to the feminine, and sensual pleasures.

◇ **Hummingbirds.** A reminder of the joy and sweetness in my heart and to be present with where it wants to lead me.

◇ **Lavender color in the aura.** Energetic sensitivities. This is often the color of a highly sensitive person, who sometimes fears their sensitivities.

◇ **The number three.** Self-expression.

Ancestors

Ritual connects us to all who have come before, to all who have walked this sacred Earth learning the way of tending, learning their lessons of spiritual evolution and truth. All our ancestors who have come before us are guiding us in Spirit. We have ancestors so ancient, who carry so much wisdom and spiritual power, including the ancestral lineages that exist in our DNA. Even if we don't know our ancestors or where we come from, their songs hum in our bones and their wisdom flows in our blood and spirits. We only need to be open to connecting with them, using our intention, space, love, and belief. Ritual enables us to create space to connect and communicate with all of those who have come before. Ritual ties us to our ancestors in sacred threads braided across infinite time, bridging between past and future. Tending to our ancestral lineages through ritual work reminds us where we came from. They help us to honor and strengthen our connection to all the weavers and seekers and earth-tenders who got us here.

Our ancestors guide us, but we also carry them forward to the light as we connect to the Sacred on our paths, healing any of their wounding and pain by tending to our own.

ANCESTOR ALTAR

A beautiful way to honor and tend to your lineage daily is to create an ancestor altar. You can add photos, candles, fresh or dried plants or fruits from where your ancestors come from, any family memorabilia, etc. For example, my partner and I have an ancestor wall altar in the center of our home. This wall is filled with multiple generations of photos of blood ancestors, ancestral art or photos of the land, and in the center of the wall is a small shelf where we leave offerings and light candles or incense. Incense and smoke from plants calls in Spirit, so having something to burn is a beautiful way to connect. There is no right or wrong way to set this up, but you'll feel when it's complete, even if it's just one item. If you are open and present, you may feel your ancestors near. Don't fear their love and support.

When you feel called, sit or stand at your altar and commune with those who came before by leaving an offering, doing a ritual, journaling or writing a letter to an ancestor, praying, or simply drinking tea and admiring their photos. Taking time to center and heal yourself while honoring your ancestors is a wonderful practice to guide you through your days with their loving support. Making an offering of water to your ancestors is another way to encourage collective healing, as the shadows that come up for us have often been passed down for generations.

It is also important to understand the expansiveness of our spirit beyond the identity of recent family histories. We also have a powerful line of ancestors that go back to the beginning of our species and beyond. Even ancient plants and animals may be our ancestors, depending on our spirit's lineage. Once upon a time, our people weren't as separated as they are now, and humans lived among little people (faeries, gnomes, leprechauns, or whatever they are called in different parts of the world), elemental spirits, and other creatures now considered to be mythic or just the stuff of legend. Many ancestors who come to teach me are from all walks of life and arrays of bodies. So far on my path, I have connected with ancient indigenous ancestors from North America, as well as those of Asia, Africa, and Europe. I also have ancestors who are elves and flower spirits, as my own spirit is of elemental origin. The ancestors who spoke strongly to me while writing this book were from a tribe of reindeer herders in what is now Siberia. Connecting to these ancestors—especially as someone without a strong lineage bond in this lifetime—allows me to feel a sense of familiar support in my life. I also find ancestors in the ancient water of our Earth, crystals, and trees. They are all our ancestors. To me, ancestral tending means recognizing your genetic bloodline, as well as your spiritual lineage. We need to find healing in both.

Dreamweaving

Dreams are our teachers, and some of the most profound guidance we'll ever find is laced through their cosmic webs. They hold potent messages cast into images and symbols we are to decode to guide us to the root of our issues, emotions, and desires. They can teach us what we truly need, what emotions we block, what nourishment our soul asks for, and even give us hints as to what is to come. They can show us what steps to take on our path, important patterns, and what we need to process. I find that my ancestors and guides speak to me the clearest in dreams, when the mind's judgment is at rest and space for potential is most abundant.

Every morning before getting out of bed, I journal and reflect on my dreams in order to integrate their messages into my conscious awareness so that I can move forward with the wisdom gained. Dream journaling is a practice I have done since I was a little girl, as I always had profound dreams and visitors in dreamtime to support me along my path. A family member gave me a dream symbolism book not too long after I learned to read that was my first introdution to Spirit's symbolism. It was my favorite book as a child and I carried it with me until it eventually got lost in my move from New York City. Even from a young age, I was dedicated to understanding the messages coming through my dreams from Spirit.

DREAM RITUAL

Dream work offers a simple way to connect to your inner guidance and listen to the wisdom Spirit is sending through. Often, my dreams will suggest places I need to go or people I need to call, hint at which spirit beings are ready to work with me, and show me subconscious patterns that need healing attention.

Before bed, set the intention for what you would like to receive through your dream. Mine usually includes receiving messages on something I need clarity on, guidance on how to process through my healing, or anything that helps me show up in service for the Earth at this time. For light, you may also choose to only use candles in your bedroom at night to allow your body to slowly sink into its natural rhythm. You may like to drink a cup of grounding tea, do a ritual to wind you down, anoint yourself with oil, or allow yourself to fall asleep without any screens or stimulants.

If you have a hard time remembering your dreams, or just want to amplify your dream practice, place a single mugwort leaf under your pillow or waft the smoke of dried mugwort around your bed before sleeping or upon waking. Mugwort is a wise feminine medicine that assists us in attuning to the unseen. She is a plant for remembering, recalling, and rewilding—an herbal guide for journeying across the bridge into magical realms of consciousness, heightening our visions, opening portals, and grounding us into our knowing.

Set a glass of water and a notebook and pen on your bedside table before going to bed. As I've mentioned before, water acts as a conduit of energy and symbol of receptivity. Upon waking, write down every detail you can remember about your dreams—the colors, people, words, symbols, scenes, elements, numbers, and feelings. Spend time reflecting on what each means to you. Though there are countless books on dream decoding and sacred symbolism, the best guide is your own intuition. You can allow books and websites to assist you, but allow your intuition to have the final say. One thing I always like to ask my dream self is, "How was I feeling?" in order to get to the root of the message. If you struggle to remember your dreams, try connecting to the mugwort again upon waking, drop down into your center, ask your spirit to remember, and surrender your mind to simply be present and observe. Allow yourself to float back into a meditative space. You will eventually see a story form with a message of guidance for you. Feel into its wisdom and whatever the dream is telling you. Sit with what you've uncovered and allow it to sink in, thanking your guides for the messages.

It may take a few nights of practice to remember your dreams if you aren't used to dream recording. You can also try changing up your nightly ritual, remove stimulants, and avoid any substances that alter your channels. What you eat for dinner can also affect your dream life, so try out different foods, as well. Be patient, trust your process, and stay with your intention.

Past Lives

Even if we don't know where we go when we die or where we came from before we were born, we do have access to lifetimes of memories within our souls. We are all sacred spiritual beings with infinite memories and wisdom safely tucked away in our spirit, and we can access all of it. By connecting to our intuitive centers, we can access these memories and gain insights and wisdom to carry forward in our current lifetime. This is the wonderful mystery of being a spirit in human form.

I have uncovered a number of my own past lives through meditation practices, and they have taught me so much, healed imprinted wounds, and inspired wild courage and passion in my heart. I have seen lives that reminded me of my power, showed me where I still hold on to limitations or fears from that life, and even some that clarified my soul's purpose and sacred gifts. In one—uncovered a couple of months before I found my publisher and began birthing this book—I saw myself as a man in medieval France, around the same age as I am now. I was a writer who communicated with the spirits of the Earth—the gnomes, faeries, trees, and river spirits—channeling their wisdom and sharing their teachings to offer a healing balm to the world. My mission was to teach people to return to the Sacred, the Earth and all her medicine, and the ways of the heart in order to create balance and harmony on Earth. When I finished the book, I met with investors to help get my writing into the world, but I was ridiculed and laughed at. Men of material power and money called me names and told me to leave. I then began to see flashes of other lives involving the same scorn—lives in which I suffered the same ridicule and devastation whenever I tried to get my work out into the world. I felt lost and defeated. Upon walking home, I came across a young child I knew and had a close relationship with. I handed him my rolled up manuscript and told him that when the world is ready, he must share the teachings contained within, that they were important in helping to heal our world. I knew a child would be open enough to carry the wisdom forward in his heart, not yet hardened by the conditioning of the world. The child promised to keep the manuscript safe and bring its teachings forward at the right time.

I emerged from this past life vision with both pain and courage in my heart. Pain for the many lifetimes of fear and doubt I've endured from myself and others, but courage because I knew that in this life I am ready to share this wisdom with the world—the same wisdom I've been carrying in my spirit for lifetimes. The world is ready now. So many of us are now devoted to a healing that will empower us to find balance and connection within ourselves, the Earth, and each other.

This past life recall meditation helped me to heal the fear I had around not being taken seriously for my wisdom by the skeptics and fear mindset so prevalent in the world. I healed by writing this very book, and by reclaiming the part of my spirit that was afraid of being misunderstood or not listened to or valued for what I have to say, because this wisdom exists in the unseen realms. I connect to the practice of past life recall whenever I need to remember my truth and be guided by my soul's essence, as well as when I need to remember all that my soul has experienced to get to this point in its evolution, to remember my sacred limitlessness and divinity, and to connect with my inner wisdom and guidance. This practice can also open us up to having more frequent ancient memories, dreams, synchronicities, and signs that parallel our current timeline that can help us evolve on our paths.

PAST LIFE RITUAL

◇ Light a candle or some incense. You can also set the energy of your space with your favorite crystals and soothing singing bowls (or music you feel drawn to from a specific culture or time) gently playing in the background. You could also waft the smoke of mugwort around your body and space, or use another plant ally you feel intuitively connected to.

◇ Sit or lie down in a cozy position that will feel good to you for about 30-45 minutes.

◇ Close your eyes and take a deep breath, slowly filling your lungs up all the way and then releasing all the air you can, letting go of worries, tension, and stress held in your body at this time. At the bottom of your breath, after your exhale, begin to find a balance and presence with your natural breath.

◇ For protection, it is important to say a prayer and connect to the energy of divine love before opening to the record of your spirit's memories. You can imagine a bright, warm light passing through your body from the top of your head to your toes and visualize this light cocooning you in

its protective energy. You may also ask your guides for protection and help by stating your intention. Whatever practice you feel called to do, make it simple yet strong, with your intention guiding you.

◇ Now with your body, mind, and spirit in allowance, imagine yourself at the start of a tunnel, hallway, or corridor. Take a moment to note how this appears to you. Slowly walk forward, noticing the lighting, smells, colors, material objects, and other details you see in this pathway. Take each visual step with intention and close observation.

◇ At the end of your pathway you'll come to a door leading you to a past remembrance that will best guide you at this time. Notice what the door looks like.

◇ With a feeling of peace and wisdom, open the door. Allow your spirit to accept the first things you see. Maybe it's a person, a color, a scene, a room, an animal, or something else. Build upon this image by focusing your attention, holding onto the scene, and softening in order to receive any other visions and messages that wish to come through and support you in your remembrance.

◇ Be patient if you don't see anything at first. You can try scanning your appearance in this visual imagining, starting at your feet. What you are wearing can give you clues to which timeline you are exploring. No matter what, what you see holds truth and importance, so don't dismiss it or allow the analytical mind to control or doubt. Acceptance is key, and you must choose to believe if you are going to get anywhere with this practice. Simply allow each image you receive to gracefully guide you to the next.

◇ When you have received all that you wish for this round, thank your guides and return to the door you entered, opening it and slowly following the pathway back to your starting point.

◇ Take a few deep breaths and bring awareness back to your body, giving your toes a wiggle, and connect to your senses to bring you in tune with your surroundings. When you are ready, open your eyes.

◇ As soon as you can, record everything you saw with as much detail as possible in your journal or make a voice memo or video. It's important to record right away. After you have recorded you can spend time deciphering images, symbols, and messages. Allow each detail to bring you clarity about your purpose, history, ancestral karma, present, and future.

When practicing with this ritual, it is important to allow all that came through to be just as it is. Your mind may tell you that it's all your imagination, but only practice will unveil the patterns, themes, memories, and guidance you need. Reincarnation is our soul's maturing process, and we each have a unique journey. When we can learn to witness the past from our current perspective, we can use our past to make choices in the present that guide our soul forward into greater alignment. What matters is your life now, in the present. Allow the past to serve, teach, and heal, but root yourself in your current unfolding.

Communication with spirit guidance can only occur with ears that truly listen, eyes that are open to see the unseen, and hearts that are willing to witness the entire sea of reality. Ritual work is mysterious, and trust is truly our greatest ally in our sacred tending. Trust in the messages that come through for you. And remember, guidance comes in all shapes, colors, and sizes, and our journeys—past, present, and future—are all unique. We can never compare our spiritual journeys or ways of receiving the Sacred to another's path. And doubt, comparison, and judgment always come from the ego. Receive your guidance with love and gratitude, and the more you open your heart to the Sacred, the more you will receive in return.

Chapter Eighteen

Returning to Love

Before we are born into human form, we exist as infinite spirit beings of love. When we make the journey into a body and are born on this Earth, we remain that cosmic, pure being of love. Love is the only thing we know. But as we grow up and navigate the harsh realities of modernity, we get off track. Somewhere along the way, we abandoned our intuitive knowing, our spiritual power, our magic, and allowed our ego minds to run the show instead of our hearts.

Ritual can guide us home to the presence of infinite love in our hearts. In connection to this love we can remember what truly matters in this existence—we remember our purpose, our pleasure, and our passion for living. We remember the interconnectedness of all life. And that the portal to this awakening is through the heart, for love is sacred unity. To truly feel our fullest potential of love we must work through the belief that we are separate—from love, from each other, from the Earth, from Spirit, and even that our minds are separate from our hearts and that our darkness is separate from our light. When we perceive ourselves as separate, we remain separate from the potential of love available to us. In the realm of the Sacred, there is no class system, no race division, no better or less than. In the realm of the Sacred, we witness all common threads that bind us together in holy union.

One of the ways our created sense of division shows up collectively is in lack of empathy and connection. Sadly, we often don't care unless something affects us personally. This is at the root of our earthly imbalances. It is why we take from the Earth without recognizing the consequences of how it affects each and every one of us. It's the energy behind our mindless consumerism and pollution. It's why we don't all collectively come together, roll up our sleeves, and get to work to heal when something traumatic happens to our brothers and sisters in other parts of the world. It's why we judge and compare and project. It's why we sabotage, cheat, and have power struggles in relationships. It's the reason for the 1%, patriarchal control, racism, and war. It's why women have been viewed as lesser than men and undervalued for thousands of years. It fuels the borders between countries, races, and hearts. It's an epidemic that needs our healing now to restore balance on Earth. This is the most important healing work we can do in this lifetime. It's why we are here.

In order to create unity, to have peace across nations, reciprocity with our Earth Mother, and union with all that is sacred, we must start with self-union. The greatest service we can be to the collective and the Earth is to do our inner shadow work and show up in union with the self, so we can show up exactly the way the Earth needs us to—exactly in harmony with why our soul came here. The Earth called us here for this very reason—to heal dense karma that has been building up generation after generation and attacking the Earth and her children. When we can each individually heal the belief of separation in ourselves, learning to see all as sacred and one from the heart, we can find harmony in our existence on this planet. This collective healing can truly end wars and heal our planet.

It won't be easy. It takes more than "love and light," positive thinking, and meditation to achieve enlightenment, as we have often seen modeled in modern spiritual communities. Yes, we can mentally understand this perspective of love and oneness and begin to see the unified nature of all. Yes, we can focus on the positive. However, if we are still judging ourselves or judging anyone else—whether a stranger or family member, whether consciously or subconsciously—we can't genuinely project love and oneness into the collective. If we don't face the shadows within and integrate them with love, we cannot experience true unity. We must do the messy and painful shadow work and face what is hidden in order to embody the light.

This energy of separation has been a huge block in our collective for thousands and thousands of years, driven by fear of what we cannot see or control, and carried forward generation after generation as the energies accumulate. We collectively lean on judgment as a form of protection and control in our separation to feel superior, fueled by our fears and doubts. We are afraid to go into our lunar selves—our shadows—and actually face what we need to witness and heal. And these days, judgment seems almost unavoidable with social media, celebrity culture, and various industries deciding what is beautiful and worthy, and the government determining our value based on our beliefs and color of our skin. The energy of fear generated and perpetuated by the patriarchy wants us to feel small and unimportant so they can remain in power and control. That's why we all need to look within and radically return to embodying the love that we are, so that we can finally claim spiritual sovereignty.

To truly embody unity, we have to start with recognizing the unity in ourselves and seeing ourselves with sacred wholeness for the beings of love that we are—including all of our flaws, wounds, wrongdoings, ancestral wounds, and shadows. From this place, we can begin to see all as one in return. Healing judgment from within is what can bring us home to recognizing the sacred love within, enabling us to see that love reflected in external reality. At the root, it is really only love we are separate from.

You can heal the fear that causes that separation with many of the tools you have gained through your journey with this book. When you notice comparison, judgment, lack of empathy and compassion for others or yourself, or the energy of separation come up for you in any way—whether with a partner, a group of people, or Spirit—anchor into the four pillars of your ritual practice.

Whether it's the Ritual to Open to Love in chapter one or the Self-Forgiveness Ritual in chapter twelve, whatever brings you back to love, do it, and often. Every day, wake up and commit to love. Allow ritual to set you free, heal your wounds, and assist you in letting go of all resentments, judgments, jealousies, and fear. Allow ritual to teach you to see yourself and others with fresh eyes—free of judgment, triggers, and shame, with only love in the present beating of your sacred heart. Allow yourself to heal all limiting beliefs (see the Ritual for Removing Limiting Beliefs in chapter one) that keep you from love, knowing that with this healing, you are actively doing the necessary work to lead our collective back to unity. This healing takes each and every one of us.

The energy of separateness and the lack of self-unity also results in the idea that we are all meant to be the same, act the same, and look the same. The idea of controlled sameness is celebrated in our culture and passed down from generation to generation in order to keep us small, controlled, and disconnected from our hearts. Speaking, acting, being, and creating as others do does not lead to liberation, truth, peace, joy, or collective unity. The patriarchal paradigm doesn't want us to know how successful, aligned, and happy we all can be if we honor our uniqueness, stand true in what makes us one of a kind, and learn to accept others for their uniqueness, as well. Every person has their own flavor of magic, beauty, gifts to offer the world and unique way of expressing them, and this life is designed to support all of us equally to reach that expression at its fullest. Whatever your talent, gift, expertise, and wisdom is, the world needs it. This is your medicine.

We are all spiritual beings here on this Earth healing, growing, and awakening. No one is more powerful than another or more worthy. No one is more spiritual or more important. We are all given what we need to grow to align with this unique expression of our magic, and our paths will show each of us what we need to heal and evolve to move in alignment with all that is sacred. We all hold the power to change the world and lift the gates of oppression. Allow your power and wisdom to be free, to ripple out into the sea of collective becoming, and to surge us back to love. We change the old paradigm through our direct connection to our love, returning to its sacred power. We're all in this together, feeling through these waves of healing in different ways. Let us remember to give selflessly and unconditionally, and to receive wholeheartedly, recognizing all as one.

As we swim through the powerful changes that are unfolding collectively, may we surrender to the unknown and find loving strength in the Sacred. May we trust ourselves as we flow through these wild waters of life, not needing to know all the answers, but listening to the wisdom of the wind in each moment. Let us create a world together that encourages the flow of our hearts, deepening intimacy with all life and each other.

Letting Go of Control

Control resists the flowing softness that guides the natural balance of life. You can't control the way a wild plant wants to grow, or the way a bird flies. You can't control sun rises, the moon's phases, or any other rhythm of life. It's important to learn to let go of control on our sacred paths, detach from plans of the mind, and allow space for things to shift, grow, and expand into something greater than our minds can even perceive. Ritual allows us to create space for intention, space, love, and belief in order to surrender control to the Universe and trust in the Sacred. Relinquishing control and becoming more receptive actually brings in much ease, prosperity, and love into our lives—all without effort. This is not about being passive, but finding sacred balance between the feminine and masculine within, and allowing our hearts to be open and trusting while committing to our sacred paths.

This path of sacred tending asks us to make countless leaps of faith and follow our intuition even when it makes no sense. It means letting go of future projections and focusing on the present moment, and following our passions even when we are told we won't be successful by doing so. It means trusting what you cannot see, and all you have no worldly evidence to prove. This path asks us to believe in ourselves, even when the world does not. The Sacred is always placing its trust in us—we only need to let go of control and follow the sacred beating of our hearts, the whispers of the wind, sacred guidance of Spirit, and all the Universe's magic.

Control from society, family, religion, and limiting beliefs also disconnect us from the potential of our love. I have always been a rebel with a fear of control that spans lifetimes, giving me the courage to work hard to go against anything that feels controlling and confining to my spirit. Although it's made me the outsider and black sheep of my family—the strange one with a knowing and gifts most can't understand or put a label on—honoring the freedom to follow my truth instead of the control and limitations of the world has made me a visionary and pioneer in my career and communities. Staying true to my heart led me to my true family and my dreams, and it is ultimately leading my lineage to a higher consciousness. I would not have written this book had I followed the rules, projected fears, and limitations imposed and laid out before me.

It is okay to be different. It is okay to go in the opposite direction of what you were told by those trying to control your path. Never conform to try to fit in. Pave your own pathway. Be different and honor what makes you unique. The more we hide

ourselves and tuck away our truth so that we can feel liked or understood (in the way culture has told us to be), the more we deprive ourselves from embodying the expression of who our unique souls came here to be, which (hint!) is not to be like anyone else! Stepping away from the norm is what turns one into a leader for others. It's what will encourage them to do the same, ultimately changing our collective ways of being—all the habits and patterns that have not been working for our evolution.

Be the rebel, the shapeshifter, the one with a different set of beliefs and unique wisdom pulsing through you, the one who communicates with Spirit, and the one who is guided by the heart over the mind. Be the healer, the visionary, the artist, the creator of your sacred life, fueled by your sacred love that knows no bounds. You are here to be different for a reason—to lead our collective sameness into the new paradigm of honoring limitless individuality and all as sacred.

LETTING GO RITUAL

Here's a way to alchemize a ritual scrub in order to shed whatever controls are holding you back and refresh your spirit as you make space to be free.

◇ In a cup or jar, combine 1 tablespoon of dried rosemary sprigs (which are grounding and will invite in peace, protection, and cleansing to release unwanted energies), 1 tablespoon of dried rose petals (nourishing to the heart and helpful in raising your vibration to match the energy of pure love), 1/2 cup of sea salt (cleansing, healing, protecting), 1 tablespoon of green clay (detoxifying), and 1/4 cup olive oil (nourishing, healing).

◇ Shake or stir while setting intentions to release control.

◇ Create sacred space in your tub, shower, or outside on the Earth and apply it to any area of your body where you feel tension or intuitively feel you are holding onto any control keeping you from expansion. Allow the medicine of the plants to wash over you as you intentionally work them into your skin.

◇ Allow the scrub to sit for a few moments. During this time you may wish to meditate, breathe deeply, visualize, hum, or sing.

◇ When you are ready, slowly and mindfully rinse off. As you rinse, imagine dense energy of control melting off your body, recycling back into the Earth, and being replaced with peace, love, and trust.

◇ Thank your body, the plants, and your spirit for this transformation, and allow your energy to open to truth.

Liberation

As we grow on our paths and return to the sacred love within, we will face a number of tasks that require us to step outside our comfort zones. That's where the deepest fulfillment lives, just beyond the threshold of "security" into the magic of blissful pleasure fueled by wild surrender. Fear is the only thing that stops us from entering full liberation along our paths. If this is challenging for you, practice the ritual of intentionally doing something outside of your comfort zone—go to a coffee shop in a different neighborhood, attend an event where you don't know anyone, quit the job you hate to follow your dreams. Whenever you choose to do something radically different and cross the line from fear to liberation, the magic happens and the real healing begins.

Because of my upbringing, being open to receiving love was always a challenge. I often didn't feel secure in romantic or intimate relationships, because I didn't feel safe, loved unconditionally, or supported by my parents as a child. For much of my life I would close off, shut down, let my ego mind and fear run the show—anything that kept me hidden from the potential of being hurt by love's power. Part of this was because deep down I didn't feel worthy of the love I wanted, but I also was afraid that the love would come with conditions, because that's how I witnessed love growing up.

I think this pattern is common for most people. I think we so often believe that love always comes with pain, and that's why we fear having an open heart to love. But we forget that even pain comes from the source of love. It is our fear built up in layers around our hearts that holds onto our pain, and when the heart is challenged to open, those layers must begin to shed. And resistance is a natural human response to what we believe will cause us pain, discomfort, or change, so it's not always easy to let our hearts be free to love in all their expanse. Meeting my partner—who has given me the purest love since the day we met—made opening to love quite the uncomfortable and painful challenge, because my ego and shadow wounds tried to fight love's warm embrace. But doing so transformed my entire life. This relationship was a big catalyst that propelled me toward all my desires, because it opened me wide.

Love asks you to do the inner work, to stay open, available, trusting, and committed to its energy every single day. Since opening to a greater love through my relationship, my life path has expanded in wildly expedited ways. My reality quickly became a reflection of what I was now present to in my heart: truth, passion, love, receptivity, connection, meaning, purpose. My career instantly took off at rapid speed, I met my soul family members, all my desires started flying at me, I left New York City (which was too stimulating for me), traveled the world with fully booked residencies for my Soul Tattoo® sessions, got a literary agent, then a dream publisher, moved to an idyllic country house tucked away in the redwoods on the Mendocino Coast, stepped into an expansive teaching partnership, birthed new projects in alignment with my deepest passions, and eventually married my love as I stepped beyond my fears and opened more and more to love's embrace. Love gave me the freedom I always desired. And that's exactly what love is—liberation.

Nothing we desire can come to us without the pure and authentic energy of love. It is our love—our commitment to its holy power—that leads us to liberation. Don't let your fear control you and hold you back from receiving all the love that is your birthright. The prayer below is my favorite to call upon when I feel fear creeping in and preventing me from expanding and surrendering to what love is guiding me into. Repeat it three times with your hands on your heart.

It is safe for me to leap into the unknown and to change with courage in my heart. I lay my trust in the Divine's hands to guide me toward love into my greatest freedom.

Chapter Nineteen

Integration

The spiritual journey is just that—a journey. It's nonlinear and cannot be controlled, planned, or timed. It's a spiral, a rolling river, a wind that catches the ocean's wild current and then lands on gentle shores before taking off again, sending the sand in swirls. It takes a dedication to patience—a slow and steady wade through the wells of our heart. We can't force ourselves forward on this path, push to reach any certain destination, or will things to happen before they are aligned. The spiritual path requires trust, presence, patience, enduring love of your vessel and your spirit, and the willingness to keep on growing, walking through shadow, and blossoming through it all with courage, gratitude, and grace.

This is a journey of unbecoming in order to become. As I pointed out before, it's not just crystals and love and light. You'll need intention, an unconditional and open-hearted love, the space to commit and to grow, and a trust in the Sacred beyond all limits. Wisdom along your path comes from the deep undoing, the shadow walk. It's discovered in the darkness and the sorrow, as well as the beauty. It is found in the vine of love spiraling around your body that awakens you to your sacred essence. It takes root in us in the moments when we give ourselves the space to pause and come home to ourselves and reflect on all the moments that led us to this present space. These moments in which to root down in ourselves are the moments that truly remind us that all life is meditation. All life is a ceremony of becoming. All life is love.

When we heal and come home to the heart, we vibrationally upgrade. If we go into ritual with the intention to heal and expand—with love in our hearts, with belief, and with the space for change—it will set us up for unlimited possibilities. Something happens when we make space and set the intention to heal. It's powerful, but we can't always understand it with the mind. For this reason alone, it is important to take time to integrate all that we are growing through—new awarenesses, insights, changes, contractions, and expansions. We can integrate by simply pausing to process in the heart and body, to sit with and reflect on all that we are growing through and all the new information coming into our awareness. When we don't slow down to integrate and hold space for our growth, we often become overcome with feelings of overwhelm, fatigue, illness, confusion, and painful body ailments as energy is shifting. Often these emerge to let us know it is time to rest and detoxify from the energies we are releasing.

Our bodies will always regenerate and heal, but holding space for this process actually speeds up our healing. Our bodies operate at a slower vibration than our minds do. They need rest, time, and space to integrate. When we create space to go within and process and integrate, we allow ourselves to honor all that we have moved through, and we open to the guidance of our intuitive wisdom. We allow all the healings and teachings to catch up with us, and we give ourselves the space to move into wholeness.

Healing requires us to make space for it. We cannot heal when we're moving a million miles an hour, working a full-time job that doesn't light us up, and slogging through endless to-do lists without taking pauses for ourselves and our ritual practices. Sacred pauses are where the deep work is done. Personally, when I am going through significant spiritual upgrades or having a lot of energy release in my life, if I don't take enough time to rest and integrate, I almost always get sick in some way—a little cold, fever, aches, and pains that leave me wanting to do nothing but soak in a bath and rest. This is a type of ascension sickness—our body's way of detoxifying lower vibrational energies that no longer serve our evolution. What goes in must always come out.

When I received my first Reiki attunement, I was bedridden with a high fever, body aches, emotions all over the place, and anxiety. All my energy was detoxifying—big time. This lasted a week, but when I eventually emerged from my bed, my intuitive gifts were heightened, I experienced profound clarity, and decided I was ready to tell my boyfriend (my now husband) that I loved him and become more open about my gifts to the world. My heart was open, my channels were open, and I could feel my limiting beliefs and fears dissolving. Anytime I get sick, I know it is a sign of an energy upgrade, and I must tend to my evolution, letting it all move through me.

Sickness can be profoundly purifying in this way. You can think of this purification process like what happens when you create a new exercise routine. The new activity may cause fatigue and sore-ness for a while until your body heals itself and gains the strength it needs to sustain this new activity. But eventually, you become stronger, clearer, more balanced, and overall feel better in all ways.

Detoxification is an essential part of our spiritual journey. Depending on what we are holding onto, this will manifest in different ways but always will involve pausing, resting, and tending to ourselves as our energy purifies. Rest is like emotional surgery and can heal so much on its own. When I finish a session with a client, one of the first things I tell them is to eat healthy—avoid sugar, caffeine, alcohol, or anything else they may be sensitive to—and to take time alone, draw a warm salt bath, rest, and reflect. This is what I recommend to anyone and everyone after any healing work, whether it be a self-healing ritual or with a healer. You can honor this detoxification process by listening to your body's needs and tending to yourself with love and care.

Integration allows us to collect and reclaim parts of us we have lost, bridges the gap from our hearts to our minds, and gives us space to witness the subtle shifts we create through our ritual practices. If we don't pause to witness from our hearts, we may not be able to witness all that is changing within. If you are moving through any new awarenesses or transformations that feel a little uncomfortable—whether they are emotional, mental, or physical—take a pause to reflect and integrate all that is shifting and expanding in your world so that you can move into a greater state of balance and ease. Plant your feet firmly on the ground, but expand your awareness to experience all that life has to offer. The more you grow, the more you must root and spend time grounding down and nourishing the body. Always after healing and ritual work, drink lots and lots of water, connect to the Earth, rest, reflect, and love yourself through your changes.

RITUAL FOR INTEGRATION

Take at least ten minutes today to sit quietly, take deep breaths, clear your mind, and go within your center— that space of stillness within. Connect to your plant allies and spirit guides, calling them in for support and grounding. Set your intention for integration while placing a few drops of your favorite oil in your hands, rubbing them together to generate energy. With your hands on your heart, ask your heart to remember its potential. With your hands on your head, ask your mind to remember to find peace within yourself and trust that all is unfolding in the way it is meant to. With your hands rubbing your feet, ask your body to carry you forward into the next step in your growth process. With your hands on your lower belly, ask your spirit to light the way. Feel yourself come into a state of wholeness and remember the wisdom in your being, lovingly leading you toward your awakening. Take space to light a candle or some incense, and journal out all your recent discoveries and emotions to further process and integrate all you have learned through your recent healings and awakenings.

Honoring All Paths

Our sacred journeys will all be different. They will be on different timelines, in different orders, with different tools, come with different challenges, and present different roles. This is why it is so important to not compare or judge our path with another's. As you navigate your sacred path, you may find people who are not yet open to their love and challenge your ways of being. While the end goal is to have all hearts open and all humans tending to all that is sacred, it isn't our current reality yet. Regardless, it's important to accept people for who they are today, especially family and those who we are karmically linked to. We can't change people or force them to see a truth that they are not ready to see. The most graceful way to navigate these challenges is to lovingly lead by example—not forcing anyone onto a path of ritual or sacred tending, but shining the light of your love for all to see and leading your life as an example of sacred love in motion. By doing your work, you become the seed that sprouts in all hearts you share space with along your path.

Spirituality is not something we can collect, buy, or give to another—it must be felt from within. Just as a church is not its stained glass or arches, but the faith that blossoms within it upon soil of tended hearts. When we shine our love to others, it can open their hearts to receive love. Sharing love, being love, expressing love, and opening to love. This is the healing gift we can offer the world.

Accept that your journey may look different from that of the people in your life. Accept where you are at each day on your path as you wind through your river of life. Surrender to trust, anchored into knowing that the things we desire will happen when they are most aligned. Everything that we call in—all the changes we make, all the healing we move through—takes time. It will take as long as it needs to take. You may have to place your healing attention toward self-forgiveness again and again for years and years until the energy releases fully into unconditional self-love. Healing work is subtle and we mustn't give up. We must continue to go deeper and deeper into our hearts. To anchor within we must let go of waiting for confirmation and throw away useless atlases and how-to manuals, naming ourselves as our only authority, listening and being guided by the rhythms of our sacred hearts.

Coming Home

On your journey home to love, you will have good days and you will have hard days. This is a part of the very fabric of the Universe, both light and shadow. The goal is to be present with yourself as your needs and desires shift. Finding home within is work—extremely hard work at times while we dig through the attics of our mind, our karma, intergenerational traumas, and toss out fears and fight the currents of our pain, shadows, and wounding. The healing path can also be isolating at times. We don't always want to show our vulnerability and pain to the world, nor do we always need to, but we do need people. Our paths home to our heart require us to let go of fear and ask for support, to accept help and shoulders to lean on in times of need, whether from a therapist or a family member.

Vulnerability is strength. Our hearts need to be open to heal. The one thing we want to avoid is numbing our pain. Drugs and alcohol are common methods for numbing, but so is food, TV, social media, and even certain relationships and habits. Numbing only prevents healing and creates further repression. In difficult moments we can instead focus on small pleasures to comfort us, doing things that excite us, make us laugh and smile, and even treating ourselves in some way—a massage, self-care ritual, time to freely create, our favorite meal, or getting ourselves a small gift. When things are difficult, I remind myself that love is resilient. Love transcends all.

Always take inventory of anywhere in your life where you are not honoring your sacred heart and all its sacred love. This will guide you toward the specific rituals to connect to. Maybe your work today is in healing from pleasing others before yourself (lack of self-love), from honoring the mind over feelings and intuition (lack of self-trust), or from anything else that feels depleting to your love light. Make a pact to your heart to remove any elements that are too limiting for your powerful love. In doing so, you will find home within yourself, always remembering that within the scared beating of your heart, you are home.

RESILIENCE MIST

I recommend using this mist in ritual as a reminder of the courage and power of your love—your sacred home within.

◇ In a glass spray bottle combine 1 part spring water, 1 part rose water, a pinch of sea salt, and a dash of 30-40% drinking alcohol to preserve (about 1/2-1 teaspoon).

◇ Add in a few petals (or flower essence drops) from a sunflower, a dandelion flower, 1-2 whole borage flowers, and a sprig of fir tip or pine needle.

◇ Shake, swirl, or stir and set your intention for the mist, for it to help you call upon the courage of your love as you move through your journey. You may wish to charge your mist under the sun or full moon light for a few hours overnight.

◇ When you feel depleted, disconnected, or discouraged, spray this mist generously around your auric body.

◇ As you spray, recognize your love-light—the fiery golden light of your beating heart. Feel it pulsing through your veins. Let your light of love be a mirror to reflect the beauty of your truth—the house of love that lives within the lining of your skin.

◇ Store your spray in the fridge to prolong its life, blessing it with your love and intention each time you grab it.

Chapter Twenty

Gratitude

I t's easy to focus on all the things going wrong in life—our struggles, our pain—both individually and collectively. Sometimes we miss out on recognizing all that we have to be grateful for, even for simply being alive with a heart that beats and a will to heal, evolve, and love. Remember to express gratitude for all that you have, all that you are, and all that you are becoming.

When we take the time to express gratitude, our hearts open to allow more blessings to flow in, which gives us even more to feel grateful for. Gratitude aligns us with our high hearts and shows us the potential for living with the most love and joy possible. Always remember to express a thousand *thank yous* for the blessings received that show us we are held by the light of love every single day. Remind yourself that you are enough, that you always will be, and that you will always have enough. Having a daily gratitude practice instantly shifts our vibration to align us with the sacredness of love in our lives.

Writing your gratitude in your journal, recording it into your phone, or reciting it out loud with intention are all ways to offer a beautiful heart opening gift to yourself and Spirit each day. It is also a wonderful practice to tend to relationships with others. When making a gratitude list, just remember to really take the space to feel gratitude for the things you are listing. Don't just write them down and think them. When I do this in my personal practice, I simply place my hand on my heart and imagine that thing, person, or feeling I am grateful for. This usually opens my heart to tears that cleanse my spirit and water the Earth, or calls upon joy, bliss, or laughter. It feels so good and so beautiful to feel the expanse of gratitude within the heart.

Be grateful in your own way for your body, your spirit, the hum of your heart, the love song that changes throughout your days. Be grateful for your resilience and dedication to your path, for being the force of nature that you are.

GRATITUDE

intimate communion with life and our earth family
songs that awaken hearts
the river that washes spirits clean
the trees that ground us into the memory of who we are
creation in all its cycles
This moment here and now
The ability to laugh, kiss, dance, soak in the sunlight
and marinate under the moonlight
The wind that feeds the fire that feeds the earth that feeds me
ou, dear reader, your guide to wholeness. You, your guide to truth
You, you heart ablaze and healing
Most of all, LOVE, the source of all that is sacred

Be grateful for your body, your spirit,
the hum of your heart, the love song
that changes as you grow
like the flower you are.
Be grateful for your resilience
and dedication to your path,
for being a powerful force of nature.

Chapter Twenty-One

From Death
Comes Life

Our paths to the Sacred can be terrifying, luring us into uncomfortable deaths of former selves so that we can open our hearts to experiencing greater love. It isn't just peaceful yoga poses and aesthetically pleasing self-care rituals that we post on social media. We will experience periods of resistance and feel the weight of fears and insecurities. We will find ourselves reacting from those fears and wounds as we fight our unraveling, clinging to old truths as a way to stay safe and attached to what is already known. We will hesitate to remove ourselves from our spaces of comfort to open up to greater possibility. We will mentally challenge our hearts with a string of shoulds and conditionings that will try to keep us from expanding. We will fight our expansion, telling ourselves that is it safer to stay small. We will experience moments of falling apart, crying on the bathroom floor in desperation and despair. We will have moments of losing ourselves, not knowing who we are or who we are becoming as we change.

It's called spiritual evolution for a reason. Evolution is a constant cycling through death and rebirth, a continuous unfolding, stripping away layers upon layers and going deeper and deeper into self in order to evolve. We tend to our evolution with our sacred tending practices, which, of course, take practice. This pathway takes commitment, prioritization, dedication, pushing through the resistance, and being okay with experiencing the energy of death as you evolve. Death is a natural part of life, and the experience of feeling through death is a natural part of our humanness. There are no quick fixes for healing and returning to love. We don't sit down to meditate once and become enlightened. You don't do a single ritual from this book and then suddenly become your Highest Self. Do we pick up a paintbrush and suddenly create a masterpiece? Do we meet someone for the first time and suddenly know everything about them? Like all authentic creation processes, this path takes time. It's a relationship of constant tending, continuously showing up for what is sacred. It's a slow unfolding—a rhythm of death and rebirth, in tune with the natural cycles of the Earth, for we are a part of her.

Tending to the Sacred requires radical trust and vulnerability. It requires showing up for ourselves, for the Sacred, for love, even through shadow and fear. It requires us to leap into the unknown, to be friends with uncertainty. It requires strength to have an open heart when society tells us vulnerability is a weakness. Above all it requires courage. It requires all of this because we are worthy of love. If you are not willing to tumble and fall and face death, risk failing, open your heart even in the face of fear, and leap into the unknown, then you cannot create new life. But I promise you that from death new life always emerges. The more we grieve, the more joy can arise. The more time we take to heal, the more presence and spiritual power we feel. You are fully equipped to handle all that life flows your way. You hold the key, the tools for sacred surrender and love. You are the gift, the magic crystal, the way-shower. You are the sacred light.

CLOSING RITUAL

As we connect to the tools and rituals that support us, the inner wisdom, and the plant and spirit allies, we will begin to soften and heal, finding our way back home. If there is any medicine in the world that can return us home to the infinite and unconditional love in our hearts—the true holy value of our souls—it is the rose. When people ask me where to start in their journey to connecting to the Earth's medicine, I almost always recommend the rose. As the highest vibrating flower, rose's energetics uplift us to align with our high hearts and pure essence of being. She teaches us to love fearlessly and unconditionally and to feel our love-light radiating within. She reminds us of all the beauty and sensual pleasure of life and brings magic to any spaces within that need it. She is my favorite symbol to use in healing and art and one of the most ancient symbols in general. Her love knows no bounds. She is the sacred feminine. Allow her sacred essence to assist in returning to your beauty-filled vessel of love.

◇ With the intention to love, to receive love, and to embody love, buy yourself a bouquet of roses.

◇ Set a rose in a vase at your altar as an offering to your ancestors and the spirit beings you walk with while singing a song from your heart.

◇ Grab a large bowl filled with water and a pinch of pink salt (this ritual is also heavenly to perform by an ocean, river, or creek).

◇ Outside on the Earth (or at home at your altar), place a few blossom ends of your roses in the water to soak for a few minutes while you further set your intention and create space within.

◇ As you set your intentions, take a moment to sit with your hands in prayer at your heart. Imagine your heart slowly opening like a rose as you breathe mindfully.

◇ Then slowly and mindfully glide the wet blossoms over your skin, starting with the soles of your feet and eventually making your way up to the top of your head, while singing, praying, or humming from your heart. Concentrate on those spaces that may need extra love and support.

◇ Lie down. With the dry blossoms, begin to arrange the petals overtop and around your body, placing them on your feet, hips, stomach, chest, neck, forehead, and so on.

◇ Breathe deeply and become receptive to the rose's healing and love.

◇ Bathe in her petals with your intention forward in your mind and heart.

◇ Stay here for as long as it feels right, allowing yourself to be still and receive.

◇ When you are finished, place the rest of the stemmed wet roses in a vase on your altar to connect to this week, and take the loose petals and make a mandala on the Earth (as in chapter nine), lovingly returning the love you received back to the Earth.

> ◇ When finished, place your hand on your heart
> and repeat "I am home" four times.

Remember, you are fully equipped to handle all that life flows your way. Remember that all life is a ceremony. Remember that you are a valuable thread in the beautiful tapestry of this life. Remember to love infinitely. Listen to music you love, be around people you love, do what you love, see love, feel love, be love. With an open heart, we can anchor in the body and live out our human experiences with more joy, passion, excitement, abundance, and, of course, more love—the sacred river that carries us home.

About the Author

Ashley River Brant is a multidimensional artist and feminine healer bringing her medicine through as the creator of Soul Tattoo®, a ceremonial intuitive tattooing modality that has gained world recognition with residencies from New Zealand to New York. Ashley is also a film photographer, illustrator, writer, teacher, and the host of Weaving Your Web podcast. Ashley uses her gifts of mediumship and connection to the loving spirits of the natural world to offer a feminine voice of healing expression for collective transformation in all her work, with ritual as the bridge that may guide us home to who we are. Ashley's intention is to support the collective in awakening to a new wave of feminine power, opening our hearts to the sacred and honoring the innate creative and intuitive power within us all so that we may heal and align with our authentic expression and soul's true essence. Ashley currently lives tucked inside a misty forest on the Mendocino Coast, California, with her partner, Andrew Brant.

About Sounds True

Sounds True is a multimedia publisher whose mission is to inspire and support personal transformation and spiritual awakening. Founded in 1985 and located in Boulder, Colorado, we work with many of the leading spiritual teachers, thinkers, healers, and visionary artists of our time. We strive with every title to preserve the essential "living wisdom" of the author or artist. It is our goal to create products that not only provide information to a reader or listener but also embody the quality of a wisdom transmission.

For those seeking genuine transformation, Sounds True is your trusted partner. At SoundsTrue.com you will find a wealth of free resources to support your journey, including exclusive weekly audio interviews, free downloads, interactive learning tools, and other special savings on all our titles.

To learn more, please visit SoundsTrue.com/freegifts or call us tollfree at 800.333.9185.